The Beginning

MY STORY

MY STORY

by Marilyn Monroe

STEIN AND DAY/*Publishers*/New York

First published in 1974
Copyright © 1974 by Milton H. Greene
Library of Congress Catalog Card No. 74-77341
All rights reserved
Designed by David Miller
Printed in the United States of America
Stein and Day/*Publishers*/Scarborough House, Briarcliff Manor, N.Y. 10510
ISBN   0-8128-1707-9

CONTENTS

MY
STORY

1

HOW I RESCUED
A WHITE
PIANO

I THOUGHT the people I lived with were my parents. I called them mama and dad. The woman said to me one day, "Don't call me mama. You're old enough to know better. I'm not related to you in any way. You just board here. Your mama's coming to see you tomorrow. You can call *her* mama if you want to."

I said, thank you. I didn't ask her about the man I called dad. He was a letter carrier. I used to sit on the edge of the bathtub in the morning and watch him shave and ask him questions—which way was east or south, or how many people there were in the world. He was the only one who had ever answered any questions I asked.

The people I had thought were my parents had children of their own. They weren't mean. They were just poor. They didn't have much to give anybody, even their own children. And there was nothing left over for me. I was seven, but I did my share of the work. I washed floors and dishes and ran errands.

My mother called for me the next day. She was a pretty woman who never smiled. I'd seen her often before, but I hadn't known quite who she was.

When I said, "Hello mama," this time, she stared at me. She had never kissed me or held me in her arms or hardly spoken to me. I didn't know anything about her then, but a few years later I learned a number of things. When I think of her now my heart hurts me twice as much as it used to when I was a little girl. It hurts me for both of us.

My mother was married at fifteen. She had two children (before me) and worked in a movie studio as a film cutter. One day she came home earlier than usual and found her young husband making love to another woman. There was a big row, and her husband banged out of the flat.

While my mother was crying over the collapse of her marriage, he sneaked back one day and kidnaped her two babies. My mother spent all her savings trying to get her children back. She hunted them for a long time. Finally she traced them to Kentucky and hitchhiked to where they were.

She was broke and with hardly any strength left when she saw her children again. They were living in a fine house. Their father was married again and well off.

She met with him but didn't ask him for anything, not even to kiss the children she had been hunting for so long. But like the mother in the movie *Stella Dallas*, she went away and left them to enjoy a happier life than she could give them.

I think it was something besides being poor that made my mother leave like that. When she saw her two children laughing and playing in a fine house among happy people she must have remembered how different it had been for her as a child. Her father had been taken away to die in a mental hospital in Patton, and her grandmother had also been taken off to the mental hospital in Norwalk to die there screaming and crazy. And her brother had killed himself. And there were other family ghosts.

So my mother came back to Hollywood without her two children and went to work as a film cutter again. I wasn't born yet.

The day my mother called for me at the letter carrier's house and took me to her rooms for a visit was the first happy day in my life that I remember.

I had visited my mother before. Being sick and unable to take care of me and keep a job, too, she paid the letter carrier five dollars a week to give me a home. Every once in a while she brought me to her rooms for a visit.

I used to be frightened when I visited her and spent most of my time in the closet of her bedroom hiding among her clothes. She seldom spoke to me except to say, "Don't make so much noise, Norma." She would say this even when I was lying in bed at night and turning the pages of a book. Even the sound of a page turning made her nervous.

There was one object in my mother's rooms that always fascinated me. It was a photograph on the wall. There were no other pictures on the walls, just this one framed photograph.

Whenever I visited my mother I would stand looking at this photograph and hold my breath for fear she would order me to stop looking. I had found out that people always ordered me to stop doing anything I like to do.

This time my mother caught me staring at the photograph but didn't scold me. Instead she lifted me up in a chair so I could see it better.

"That's your father," she said.

I felt so excited I almost fell off the chair. It felt so good to have a father, to be able to look at his picture and know I belonged to him. And what a wonderful photograph it was. He wore a slouch hat a little gaily on the side. There was a lively smile in his eyes, and he had a thin mustache like Clark Gable. I felt very warm toward the picture.

My mother said, "He was killed in an auto accident in New York City."

I believed everything people told me in that time, but I didn't believe this. I didn't believe he was run over and dead. I asked my mother what his name was. She wouldn't answer, but went into the bedroom and locked herself in.

Years later I found out what his name was, and many other things about him—how he used to live in the same apartment building where my mother lived, how they fell in love, and how he walked off and left her while I was getting born—without ever seeing me.

The strange thing was that everything I heard about him made me feel warmer toward him. The night I met his picture I dreamed of it when I fell asleep. And I dreamed of it a thousand times afterward.

That was my first happy time, finding my father's picture. And every time I remembered how he smiled and how his hat was tipped I felt warm and not alone. When I started a sort of scrapbook a year later the first picture I put in it was a photograph of Clark Gable because he looked like my father—especially the way he wore his hat and mustache.

And I used to make up daydreams, not about Mr. Gable, but about my father. When I'd be walking home from school in the rain and feeling bad I'd pretend my father was waiting for me, and that he would scold me for not having worn my rubbers. I didn't own any rubbers. Nor was the place I walked to any kind of a home. It was a place where I worked as a sort of child servant, washing dishes, clothes, floors, running errands and keeping quiet.

But in a daydream you jump over facts as easily as a cat jumps over a fence. My father would be waiting for me, I daydreamed, and I would come into the house smiling from ear to ear.

Once when I lay in a hospital after having my tonsils out and running into complications, I had a daydream that lasted a whole week without stopping. I kept bringing my father into the hospital ward and walking him to my bed while the other patients looked on with disbelief and envy at so distinguished a visitor; and I kept bending him over my bed and having him kiss my forehead and I gave him dialogue, too. "You'll be well in a few days, Norma Jean. I'm very proud of the way you're behaving, not crying all the time like other girls."

And I would ask him please to take off his hat. But I could never get him in my largest, deepest daydream to take his hat off and sit down.

When I went back to my "home," I almost got sick again. A man next door chased a dog I had loved and who had been waiting for me to come home. The dog barked because he was happy to see me. And the man started chasing him and ordering him to shut up. The man had a hoe in his hand. He swung the hoe. It hit my dog's back and cut him in half.

My mother found another couple to keep me. They

were English people and needed the five dollars a week that went with me. Also, I was large for my age and could do a lot of work.

One day my mother came to call. I was in the kitchen washing dishes. She stood looking at me without talking. When I turned around I saw there were tears in her eyes, and I was surprised.

"I'm going to build a house for you and me to live in," she said. "It's going to be painted white and have a back yard." And she went away.

It was true. My mother managed it somehow, out of savings and a loan. She built a house. The English couple and I were both taken to see it. It was small and empty but beautiful, and it was painted white.

The four of us moved in. I had a room to myself. The English couple didn't have to pay rent, just take care of me as they had done before. I worked hard, but it didn't matter. It was my first home. My mother bought furniture, a table with a white top and brown legs, chairs, beds, and curtains. I heard her say, "It's all on time, but don't worry. I'm working double shift at the studio, and I'll soon be able to pay it off."

One day a grand piano arrived at my home. It was out of condition. My mother had bought it secondhand. It was for me. I was going to be given piano lessons on it. It was a very important piano, despite being a little banged up. It had belonged to the movie star Fredric March.

"You'll play the piano over here, by the windows," my mother said, "and here on each side of the fireplace there'll be a love seat. And we can sit listening to you. As soon as I pay off a few other things I'll get the love seats, and we'll all sit in them at night and listen to you play the piano."

But the two love seats were not to be. One morning the English couple and I were having breakfast in the kitchen. It was early. Suddenly there was a terrible noise on the stairway outside the kitchen. It was the most frightening noise I'd ever heard. Bangs and thuds kept on as if they would never stop.

"Something's falling down the stairs," I said.

The Englishwoman held me from going to see. Her husband went out and after a time came back into the kitchen.

"I've sent for the police and the ambulance," he said.

I asked if it was my mother.

"Yes," he said. "But you can't see her."

I stayed in the kitchen and heard people come and try to take my mother away. Nobody wanted me to see her. Everyone said, "Just stay in the kitchen like a good girl. She's all right. Nothing serious."

But I went out and looked in the hall. My mother was on her feet. She was screaming and laughing. They took her away to the Norwalk Mental Hospital. I knew the name of the hospital in a vague way. It was where my mother's father and grandmother had been taken when they started screaming and laughing.

All the furniture disappeared. The white table, the chairs, the beds and white curtains melted away, and the grand piano, too.

The English couple disappeared also. And I was taken from the newly painted house to an orphan asylum and given a blue dress and a white shirtwaist to wear and shoes with heavy soles. And for a long time when I lay in bed at night I could no longer daydream about anything. I kept hearing the terrible noise on the stairs and my mother screaming and laughing as they led her out of the home she had tried to build for me.

I never forgot the white painted house and its furniture. Years later when I was beginning to earn some money modeling, I started looking for the Fredric March piano. After about a year I found it in an old auction room and bought it.

I have it in my home now in Hollywood. It's been painted a lovely white, and it has new strings and plays as wonderfully as any piano in the world.

Y MOTHER's best friend was a woman named
Grace. I called nearly everybody I knew Aunt or Uncle, but
Aunt Grace was a different sort of make-believe relative.
She became my best friend, too.

Aunt Grace worked as a film librarian in the same
studio as my mother—Columbia Pictures. She was the first
person who ever patted my head or touched my cheek. That
happened when I was eight. I can still remember how
thrilled I felt when her kind hand touched me.

Grace had almost as rough a time as my mother. She lost
her job in the studio and had to scrape for a living.
Although she had no money, she continued to look after
my mother who was starting to have mental spells—and to
look after me. At times she took me to live with her. When
she ran out of money and had only a half dollar left for a
week's food, we lived on stale bread and milk. You could
buy a sackful of old bread at the Holmes Bakery for
twenty-five cents. Aunt Grace and I would stand in line for
hours waiting to fill our sack. When I looked up at her she
would grin at me and say, "Don't worry, Norma Jean.
You're going to be a beautiful girl when you grow up. I can
feel it in my bones."

Her words made me so happy that the stale bread tasted
like cream puffs.

Everything seemed to go wrong for Aunt Grace. Only
bad luck and death ever visited her. But there was no
bitterness in my aunt. Her heart remained tender, and she
believed in God. Nearly everybody I knew talked to me
about God. They always warned me not to offend Him. But
when Grace talked about God, she touched my cheek and

said that He loved me and watched over me. Remembering what Grace had said I lay in bed at night crying to myself. The only One who loved me and watched over me was Someone I couldn't see or hear or touch. I used to draw pictures of God whenever I had time. In my pictures He looked a little like Aunt Grace and a little like Clark Gable.

As I grew older I knew I was different from other children because there were no kisses or promises in my life. I often felt lonely and wanted to die. I would try to cheer myself up with daydreams. I never dreamed of anyone loving me as I saw other children loved. That was too big a stretch for my imagination. I compromised by dreaming of my attracting someone's attention (besides God), of having people look at me and say my name.

This wish for attention had something to do, I think, with my trouble in church on Sundays. No sooner was I in the pew with the organ playing and everybody singing a hymn than the impulse would come to me to take off all my clothes. I wanted desperately to stand up naked for God and everyone else to see. I had to clench my teeth and sit on my hands to keep myself from undressing. Sometimes I had to pray hard and beg God to stop me from taking my clothes off.

I even had dreams about it. In the dream I entered the church wearing a hoop skirt with nothing under it. The people would be lying on their backs in the church aisle, and I would step over them, and they would look up at me.

My impulse to appear naked and my dreams about it had no shame or sense of sin in them. Dreaming of people looking at me made me feel less lonely. I think I wanted them to see me naked because I was ashamed of the clothes I wore—the never changing faded blue dress of poverty. Naked, I was like other girls and not someone in an orphan's uniform.

When my mother was taken to the hospital, Aunt Grace became my legal guardian. I could hear her friends arguing in her room at night when I lay in her bed pretending to be asleep. They advised her against adopting me because I was certain to become more and more of a responsibility as I grew older. This was on account of my "heritage," they said. They talked about my mother and her father and brother and grandmother all being mental cases and said I would certainly follow in their footsteps. I lay in bed shivering as I listened. I didn't know what a mental case was, but I knew it wasn't anything good. And I held my breath waiting to hear whether Aunt Grace would let me become a state orphan or adopt me as her own. After a few evenings of argument Aunt Grace adopted me, heritage and all, and I fell asleep happy.

Grace, my new guardian, had no money and was out looking for a job all the time, so she arranged for me to enter the Orphan Asylum—the Los Angeles Children's Home Society. I didn't mind going there because even in the orphanage I knew I had a guardian outside—Aunt Grace. It wasn't till later that I realized how much she had done for me. If not for Grace I would have been sent to a state or county institution where there are fewer privileges, such as being allowed to have a Christmas tree or seeing a movie sometimes.

I lived in the orphanage only off and on. Most of the time I was placed with a family, who were given five dollars a week for keeping me. I was placed in nine different families before I was able to quit being a legal orphan. I did this at sixteen by getting married.

The families with whom I lived had one thing in common—a need for five dollars. I was, also, an asset to have in the house. I was strong and healthy and able to do almost as much work as a grownup. And I had learned not to bother anyone by talking or crying.

I learned also that the best way to keep out of trouble was by never complaining or asking for anything. Most of the families had children of their own, and I knew they always came first. They wore the colored dresses and owned whatever toys there were, and they were the ones who were believed.

My own costume never varied. It consisted of a faded

blue skirt and white waist. I had two of each, but since they were exactly alike everyone thought I wore the same outfit all the time. It was one of the things that annoyed people—my wearing the same clothes.

Every second week the Home sent a woman inspector out to see how its orphans were getting along in the world. She never asked me any questions but would pick up my foot and look at the bottoms of my shoes. If my shoe bottoms weren't worn through, I was reported in a thriving condition.

I never minded coming "last" in these families except on Saturday nights when everybody took a bath. Water cost money, and changing the water in the tub was an unheard of extravagance. The whole family used the same tub of water. And I was always the last one in.

One family with whom I lived was so poor that I was often scolded for flushing the toilet at night.

"That uses up five gallons of water," my new "uncle" would say, "and five gallons each time can run into money. You can do the flushing in the morning."

No matter how careful I was, there were always troubles. Once in school, a little Mexican boy started howling that I had hit him. I hadn't. And I was often accused of stealing things—a necklace, a comb, a ring, or a nickel. I never stole anything.

When the troubles came I had only one way to meet them—by staying silent. Aunt Grace would ask me when she came to visit how things were. I would tell her always they were fine because I didn't like to see her eyes turn unhappy.

Some of my troubles were my own fault. I did hit someone occasionally, pull her hair, and knock her down. But worse than that were my "character faults." A slightly overgrown child who stares and hardly ever speaks, and who expects only one thing of a home—to be thrown out—can seem like a nuisance to have around.

There was one home I hoped wouldn't throw me out. This was a house with four children who were watched over by a great-grandmother who was over a hundred years old. She took care of the children by telling them blood-curdling stories about Indian massacres, scalpings, burnings at the stake, and other wild doings of her youth. She said she had been a close friend of Buffalo Bill and had fought at his side in hand-to-hand battles with the savage Redskins.

I listened to her stories with my heart in my mouth and did everything I could to make her like me. I laughed the loudest and shivered the most at her stories. But one day one of her own great-grandchildren came running to her with her dress torn from her neck. She said I had done it. I hadn't. But the old Indian-fighter wouldn't believe me, and I was sent back to the orphanage in disgrace.

Most of my troubles were of this minor sort. In a way they were not troubles at all because I was used to them. When I look back on those days I remember, in fact, that they were full of all sorts of fun and excitement. I played games in the sun and ran races. I also had daydreams, not only about my father's photograph but about many other things.

I daydreamed chiefly about beauty. I dreamed of myself becoming so beautiful that people would turn to look at me when I passed. And I dreamed of colors—scarlet, gold, green, white. I dreamed of myself walking proudly in beautiful clothes and being admired by everyone and overhearing words of praise. I made up the praises and repeated them aloud as if someone else were saying them.

Daydreaming made my work easier. When I was waiting on the table in one of the poverty stricken, unhappy homes where I lived, I would daydream I was a waitress in an elegant hotel, dressed in a white waitress uniform, and everybody who entered the grand dining room where I was serving would stop to look at me and openly admire me.

I never daydreamed about love, even after I fell in love the first time. This was when I was around eight. I fell in love with a boy named George who was a year older. We used to hide in the grass together until he got frightened and jumped up and ran away.

What we did in the grass never frightened me. I knew it was wrong, or I wouldn't have hidden, but I didn't know *what* was wrong. At night I lay awake and tried to figure out what sex was and what love was. I wanted to ask a thousand questions, but there was no one to ask. Besides I knew that people only told lies to children—lies about everything from soup to Santa Claus.

Then one day I found out about sex without asking any questions. I was almost nine, and I lived with a family that rented a room to a man named Kimmel. He was a stern looking man, and everybody respected him and called him Mr. Kimmel.

I was passing his room when his door opened and he said quietly, "Please come in here, Norma."

I thought he wanted me to run an errand.

"Where do you want me to go, Mr. Kimmel?" I asked.

"No place," he said and closed the door behind me. He smiled at me and turned the key in the lock.

"Now you can't get out," he said, as if we were playing a game.

I stood staring at him. I was frightened, but I didn't dare yell. I knew if I yelled I would be sent back to the orphanage in disgrace again. Mr. Kimmel knew this, too.

When he put his arms around me I kicked and fought as hard as I could, but I didn't make any sound. He was stronger than I was and wouldn't let me go. He kept whispering to me to be a good girl.

When he unlocked the door and let me out, I ran to tell my "aunt" what Mr. Kimmel had done.

"I want to tell you something," I stammered, "about Mr. Kimmel. He—he—"

My aunt interrupted.

"Don't you dare say anything against Mr. Kimmel," she said angrily. "Mr. Kimmel's a fine man. He's my star boarder!"

Mr. Kimmel came out of his room and stood in the doorway, smiling.

"Shame on you!" my "aunt" glared at me, "complaining about people!"

"This is different," I began, "this is something I have to tell. Mr. Kimmel—"

I started stammering again and couldn't finish. Mr. Kimmel came up to me and handed me a nickel.

"Go buy yourself some ice cream," he said.

I threw the nickel in Mr. Kimmel's face and ran out.

I cried in bed that night and wanted to die. I thought, "If there's nobody ever on my side that I can talk to I'll start screaming." But I didn't scream.

A week later the family including Mr. Kimmel went to a religious revival meeting in a tent. My "aunt" insisted I come along.

The tent was jammed. Everybody was listening to the evangelist. He was half singing and half talking about the sinfulness of the world. Suddenly he called on all the sinners in the tent to come up to the altar of God where he stood—and repent.

I rushed up ahead of everyone else and started telling about my "sin."

"On your knees, sister," he said to me.

I fell on my knees and began to tell about Mr. Kimmel and how he had molested me in his room. But other "sinners" crowded around me. They also fell on their knees and started wailing about their sins and drowned me out.

I looked back and saw Mr. Kimmel standing among the nonsinners, praying loudly and devoutly for God to forgive the sins of others.

IT HAPPENED IN
MATH CLASS

A T TWELVE I looked like a girl of seventeen. My body was developed and shapely. But no one knew this but me. I still wore the blue dress and the blouse the orphanage provided. They made me look like an overgrown lummox.

I had no money. The other girls rode to school in a bus. I had no nickel to pay for the ride. Rain or shine, I walked the two miles from my "aunt's" home to the school.

I hated the walk, I hated the school. I had no friends. The pupils seldom talked to me and never wanted me in their games. Nobody ever walked home with me or invited me to visit their homes. This was partly because I came from the poor part of the district where all the Mexicans and Japanese lived. It was also because I couldn't smile at anyone.

Once a shoemaker standing in the doorway of his shop stopped me as I was walking to school.

"What's your name?" he asked me.

"Norma," I said.

"What's your last name?" he asked.

I wouldn't give him the name I had—Norma Mortenson—because it wasn't the name of the man with the slouch hat and the Gable mustache. I didn't answer.

"You're a queer kid," the shoemaker said. "I watch you pass here every day, and I've never seen you smile. You'll never get anywhere like that."

I went on to school, hating the shoemaker.

In school the pupils often whispered about me and giggled as they stared at me. They called me dumb and made fun of my orphan's outfit. I didn't mind being thought dumb. I knew I wasn't.

One morning both my white blouses were torn, and I would be late for school if I stopped to fix them. I asked one of my "sisters" in the house if she could loan me something to wear. She was my age but smaller. She loaned me a sweater.

I arrived at school just as the math class was starting. As I walked to my seat everybody stared at me as if I had suddenly grown two heads, which in a way I had. They were under my tight sweater.

At recess a half dozen boys crowded around me. They made jokes and kept looking at my sweater as if it were a gold mine. I had known for some time that I had shapely breasts and thought nothing of the fact. The math class, however, was more impressed.

After school four boys walked home with me, wheeling their bicycles by hand. I was excited but acted as if nothing unusual were happening.

The next week the shoemaker stopped me again.

"I see you've taken my advice," he said. "You'll find you get along much better if you smile at folks."

I noticed that he, also, looked at my sweater as he talked. I hadn't given it back to my "sister" yet.

The school and the day became different after that. Girls who had brothers began inviting me to their homes, and I met their folks, too. And there were always four or five boys hanging around my house. We played games in the street and stood around talking under the trees till suppertime.

I wasn't aware of anything sexual in their new liking for me, and there were no sex thoughts in my mind. I didn't think of my body as having anything to do with sex. It was more like a friend who had mysteriously appeared in my life, a sort of magic friend. A few weeks later, I stood in front of the mirror one morning and put lipstick on my lips. I darkened my blond eyebrows. I had no money for clothes, and I had no clothes except my orphan rig and the lone sweater. The lipstick and the mascara were like clothes, however. I saw that they improved my looks as much as if I had put on a real gown.

My arrival in school with painted lips and darkened brows, and still encased in the magic sweater, started everybody buzzing. And the buzzing was not all friendly. All sorts of girls, not only thirteen-year-olds but seniors of seventeen and eighteen set up shop as my enemies. They told each other and whoever would listen that I was a drunkard and spent my nights sleeping with boys on the beach.

The scandals were lies. I didn't drink, and I didn't let any boys take liberties. And I had never been on any beach in my life. But I couldn't feel angry with the scandal-makers. Girls being jealous of me! Girls frightened of losing their boy friends because I was more attractive! These were no longer daydreams made up to hide lonely hours. They were truths!

And by summertime I had a real beau. He was twenty-one, and despite being very sophisticated he thought I was eighteen instead of thirteen. I was able to fool him by keeping my mouth shut and walking a little fancy. Since taking the math class by storm a few months ago, I had practiced walking languorously.

My sophisticated beau arrived at my home one Saturday with the news that we were going swimming. I rushed into my "sister's" room (the one who was a little smaller than me) to borrow her bathing suit. Standing in front of the bureau mirror, I spent an hour putting it on and practicing walking in it.

My beau's impatient cries finally brought me out of the bedroom in an old pair of slacks and a sweater. The bathing suit was under them.

It was a sunny day, and the sand was crowded with bathers and with mothers and their children. Despite being born and raised only a few miles from the ocean I had never seen it close up before. I stood and stared for a long time. It was like something in a dream, full of gold and lavender colors, blue and foaming white. And there was a holiday feeling in the air that surprised me. Everybody seemed to be smiling at the sky.

"Come on, let's get in," my beau commanded.

"In where?" I asked.

"In the water," he laughed, thinking I had made a joke.

I thought of my tight bathing suit. The idea of hiding myself in the water while wearing it seemed to me ridiculous. But I said nothing. I stood watching the girls and women and felt a little disappointed. I hadn't expected that half the feminine population of Los Angeles would be parading the sands with almost nothing on. I thought I'd be the only one.

My beau was getting impatient again; so I removed my slacks and sweater and stood in my skimpy suit. I thought, "I'm almost naked," and I closed my eyes and stood still.

My sophisticated boy friend had stopped nagging me. I started walking slowly across the sand. I went almost to the water's edge and then walked down the beach. The same thing happened that had happened in the math class, but on a larger scale. It was also much noisier. Young men whistled at me. Some jumped up from the sand and trotted up for a better view. Even the women stopped moving as I came nearer.

I paid no attention to the whistles and whoops. In fact, I didn't hear them. I was full of a strange feeling, as if I were two people. One of them was Norma Jean from the orphanage who belonged to nobody. The other was someone whose name I didn't know. But I knew where she belonged. She belonged to the ocean and the sky and the whole world.

UT NOTHING happened out of the great vision that smote me on the beach. I went back to my blue dress and white blouse and returned to school. But instead of learning anything I grew more and more confused. So did the school. It had no way of coping with a thirteen-year-old siren.

Why I was a siren, I hadn't the faintest idea. There were no thoughts of sex in my head. I didn't want to be kissed, and I didn't dream of being seduced by a duke or a movie star. The truth was that with all my lipstick and mascara and precocious curves, I was as unsensual as a fossil. But I seemed to affect people quite otherwise.

The boys took to wooing me as if I were the sole member of my sex in the district. Being boys, most of them were satisfied with a goodnight kiss or a confused hug in a hallway. I was able, in fact, to stand off most of the spooners entirely. Boys from fifteen to eighteen are not very persistent love-makers. I imagine that if it weren't for older women seducing them they would remain virginal just as long as girls do (if they do).

Among my suitors, however, were young men who went in for major wrestling, and now and then a bona fide wolf with a complete line of dialogue and a full set of plans. These were the easiest to duck because I didn't feel sorry for them.

The truth is I never felt offended by any of them, even the wrestlers who mussed my hair. If anything, I envied them. I would have liked to want something as much as they did. I wanted nothing. They might as well have been wooing a bear in a log.

My admirers all said the same thing in different ways. It was my fault, their wanting to kiss and hug me. Some said it was the way I looked at them—with eyes full of passion. Others said it was my voice that lured them on. Still others said I gave off vibrations that floored them. I always felt they were talking about somebody else, not me. It was like being told they were attracted to me because of my diamonds and rubies. I not only had no passion in me, I didn't even know what it meant.

I used to lie awake at night wondering why the boys came after me. I didn't want them that way. I wanted to play games in the street, not in the bedroom. Occasionally I let one of them kiss me to see if there was anything interesting in the performance. There wasn't.

I decided finally that the boys came after me because I was an orphan and had no parents to protect me or frighten them off. This decision made me cooler than ever to my train of admirers. But neither coolness nor disdain, nor "get out of here," "don't bother me," "I have no interest whatsoever in kissing with my lips open," none of my frozen attitudes changed the picture. The boys continued to come after me as if I were a vampire with a rose in my teeth.

The girl pupils were another problem but one I could understand. They disliked me more and more as I grew older. Now instead of being accused of stealing combs, nickels, or necklaces, I was accused of stealing young men.

Aunt Grace suggested a solution for my troubles.

"You ought to get married," she said.

"I'm too young," I said. I was still fifteen.

"I don't think you are," Aunt Grace laughed.

"But there's nobody wants to marry me," I said.

"Yes there is," she said.

"Who?" I asked.

"Jim," said my aunt.

Jim was Mr. Dougherty. He lived near me. He was good-looking, polite, and full grown.

"But Jim is stuck on my 'sister,'" I told her.

"It was you he took to the football game," Aunt Grace said, "not her."

"It was awful boring," I said. "He's like the others, except he's taller and more polite."

"That's a fine quality in a man," said Aunt Grace, "politeness."

The "aunt" and "uncle" with whom I was living—my ninth set of relatives—helped me make up my mind. They were going to move. This meant I'd have to go back and live in the orphanage till they unloaded me on another family.

I married Jim Dougherty.

It was like being retired to a zoo.

The first effect marriage had on me was to increase my lack of interest in sex. My husband either didn't mind this or wasn't aware of it. We were both too young to discuss such an embarrassing topic openly.

Actually our marriage was a sort of friendship with sexual privileges. I found out later that marriages are often no more than that. And that husbands are chiefly good as lovers when they are betraying their wives.

Jim's folks didn't care much for me, for which I couldn't blame them. I was a peculiar wife. I disliked grownups. I preferred washing dishes to sitting and talking to them. As soon as they started playing cards or having arguments I would sneak out of the house and join the kids in the street. I liked boys and girls younger than me. I played games with them until my husband came out and started calling me to go to bed.

My marriage brought me neither happiness nor pain. My husband and I hardly spoke to each other. This wasn't because we were angry. We had nothing to say. I've seen many married couples since that were just like Jim and me. They were usually more enduring kind of marriages, the ones that were pickled in silence.

The most important thing my marriage did for me was to end forever my status as orphan. I felt grateful to Jim for this. He was the Lochinvar who had rescued me from my blue dress and white blouse.

My various advisers had been right about marriage putting an end to my popularity as a siren. The boys did not come after Mrs. Dougherty. The rose seemed to have fallen out of her teeth.

J

IM JOINED the Merchant Marine in 1944, and I went to work in a parachute factory. The great war was on. Battles were being fought. Juke boxes were playing. People's eyes were lit up.

I wore overalls in the factory. I was surprised that they insisted on this. Putting a girl in overalls is like having her work in tights, particularly if a girl knows how to wear them. As parachute inspector I was back in math class again. The men buzzed around me just as the high school boys had done.

I have noticed since that men usually leave married women alone, and are inclined to treat all wives with respect. This is no great credit to married women. Men are always ready to respect anything that bores them. The reason most wives, even pretty ones, wear such a dull look is because they're respected so much.

Maybe it was my fault that the men in the factory tried to date me and buy me drinks. I didn't feel like a married woman. I was completely faithful to my overseas husband, but that wasn't because I loved him or even because I had moral ideas. My fidelity was due to my lack of interest in sex.

Jim finally came home, and we lived together again. It's hard to remember what you said, did, or felt when you were bored.

Jim was a nice husband. He never hurt me or upset me—except on one subject. He wanted a baby.

The thought of having a baby stood my hair on end. I could see it only as myself, another Norma Jean in an orphanage. Something would happen to me. Jim would wander off. And there would be this little girl in the blue dress and white blouse living in her "aunt's" home, washing dishes, being last in the bath water on Saturday night.

I couldn't explain this to Jim. After he fell asleep beside me at night I would lie awake crying. I didn't quite know who it was that cried, Mrs. Dougherty or the child she might have. It was neither. It was Norma Jean, still alive, still alone, still wishing she were dead.

I feel different about having a child now. It's one of the things I dream of. She won't be any Norma Jean now. And I know how I'll bring her up—without lies. Nobody will tell her lies about anything. And I'll answer all her questions. If I don't know the answers I'll go to an encyclopedia and look them up. I'll tell her whatever she wants to know—about love, about sex, about everything!

But chiefly, no lies! No lies about there being a Santa Claus or about the world being full of noble and honorable people all eager to help each other and do good to each other. I'll tell her there are honor and goodness in the world, the same as there are diamonds and radium.

This is the end of my story of Norma Jean. Jim and I were divorced. And I moved into a room in Hollywood to live by myself. I was nineteen, and I wanted to find out who I was.

When I just wrote "this is the end of Norma Jean," I blushed as if I had been caught in a lie. Because this sad, bitter child who grew up too fast is hardly ever out of my heart. With success all around me, I can still feel her frightened eyes looking out of mine. She keeps saying, "I never lived, I was never loved," and often I get confused and think it's I who am saying it.

I HAD BEEN a sort of "child bride." Now I was a sort of "child widow." Many things seemed to have happened to me. Yet, in a way, nothing had happened, except that I was nineteen instead of nine, and I had to look for my own job.

The sort of instinct that leads a duck to water led me to photographer studios. I got jobs posing for ads and layouts. The chief trouble was that the photographers were also looking for work. Finding a photographer who wanted me as a model was easier than finding one who could pay more than promises.

But I made enough money for room rent and a meal a day although sometimes I fell behind on my eating. It didn't matter, though. When you're young and healthy a little hunger isn't too important.

What mattered more was being lonely. When you're young and healthy loneliness can seem more important than it is.

I looked at the streets with lonely eyes. I had no relatives to visit or chums to go places with.

My Aunt Grace and Aunt Anna were working hard to keep food in their kitchens and the rent paid. When I called on them they felt sorry for me and wanted to help me. I knew how they needed the half dollars in their purses; so I stayed away unless I had money and could take them to a restaurant or the movies.

I had only myself. When I walked home from the restaurant in the evening with the streets lighted up and a crowd on the sidewalks, I used to watch the faces chatting to each other and hurrying someplace. I wondered where they were going and how it felt to have places to go to or people who knew you.

There were always men willing to help a girl be less lonely. They said, "Hi, baby," when you passed. When you didn't turn to look at them they sneered, "Stuck up, eh?"

Sometimes they followed you and kept up a one-sided conversation. "You look all right, baby. How about we drop in someplace for a drink and a dance." After a half block when you didn't answer them, they got indignant and swore at you and dismissed you with a final insult.

I never answered them. Sometimes I felt sorry for them. They seemed as lonely as I was. It wasn't any moral attitude that kept me from accepting their sidewalk invitations. It was not wanting to be used by others. Norma Jean had been used, told to do this, do that, come here, clean the kitchen, and keep her mouth shut no matter what she felt. Everybody had had the drop on Norma Jean. If she didn't obey, back she went to the orphanage.

These lonely street corner wolves "hi-babying" me sounded like voices out of the past calling me to be Miss Nobody again—to be used and ignored.

One evening I met a man in a restaurant. We walked out of the place together, and he kept talking to me in the street. He was the first person who had talked to me for quite a while, and I listened eagerly.

"This town has sure changed a lot in the last forty years," he said. "Used to be Indians right where we're walking. All this was a kind of desert. You had to ride a horse to get anywhere."

"Did you used to live here forty years ago?" I asked.

"Yes, ma'am," he said. "How old do you think I am?"

"About sixty," I said.

"Seventy-seven my last birthday," he corrected me. "The name is Bill Cox. You going anywhere?"

I said I wasn't.

"Why not drop in on me and the missus?" he said. "Live right near here. She didn't feel in the mood for night life, so I'm bringing her home a sandwich."

I became a friend of Bill Cox and his wife. The three of us would walk together in the streets at night sometimes, but more often just Bill and I would promenade. He talked chiefly about the Spanish-American War in which he had been a soldier and about Abraham Lincoln. These two topics were very exciting to him.

I had never heard of the Spanish-American War. I must have been absent from school the week it was studied by my history class.

Bill Cox explained the whole war to me, its causes and all its battles. And he also told me the life of Abraham Lincoln from his birth onward. Walking with Bill Cox in the lighted Hollywood streets and hearing stories about the Spanish-American War and Abraham Lincoln, I didn't feel lonely and the sidewalk wolves didn't "hi-baby" me.

One evening Bill Cox told me he was going back to Texas.

"I'm feeling a little sick," he said, "and I'd hate to die anyplace except in Texas."

He sent me a few letters from Texas. I answered them. Then a letter came from his wife saying Bill Cox had died in an old soldiers' home in Texas. I read the letter in the restaurant where I had met him and walked home crying. The Hollywood streets seemed lonelier than ever without Bill Cox and San Juan and Abraham Lincoln.

UNDAYS WERE the loneliest. You couldn't look for a job on Sundays or pretend you were shopping in stores. All you could do was walk as if you were going someplace.

On one of these walks I discovered a place to go on Sundays. It was the Union Station. All the trains from all over the country came in at the Union Station. It was a beautiful building, and it was always crowded with people carrying suitcases and babies.

After that, I used to go there on Sundays and stay most of the day. I would watch people greeting each other when the train crowds entered the waiting room. Or saying good-bye to each other.

They seemed to be mostly poor people. Although now and then some well-dressed travelers would appear. But chiefly it was the poor people who kept coming in and going away on trains.

You learned a lot watching them. You learned that pretty wives adored homely men and good-looking men adored homely wives. And that people in shabby clothes, carrying raggedy bundles and with three or four sticky kids clinging to them, had faces that could light up like Christmas trees when they saw each other. And you watched really homely men and women, fat ones and old ones, kiss each other as tenderly as if they were lovers in a movie.

In addition to the Union Station, there were street corner meetings to attend. These were usually of a religious nature.

I used to stand for hours listening to the minister talking from a box. I noticed it was never really a soap box but usually an empty soft drink crate on which he stood.

The talk would be about God and the minister would call on his listeners to give Him their souls and their love.

I watched the faces of the listeners when the minister would cry out how much God loved them and how much they needed to set themselves right with God. They were faces without any argument in them, just tired faces that were glad to hear Somebody loved them.

When it came time to take up the collection I usually slipped away. I usually didn't have even a dime in my purse for carfare. Sometimes, however, I felt flush enough to drop a half dollar in the collection hat.

I got in the habit of not making up my face on Sundays or combing my hair or wearing stockings. I felt I fitted in better that way with the people in the Union Station and at the corner meetings. As for clothes, I didn't have to worry about being overdressed.

One Sunday morning I was walking in one of the streets near the Union Station looking for a meeting to attend, when a young man in a soldier's coat greeted me.

"Help the disabled war veterans," he said. "Give the crippled war heroes a chance for recovery."

He was carrying a box full of cards with small tin stars pinned on them.

"Five silver stars for fifty cents," he said. "Buy them to give to your friends to remind them of our wounded veterans."

I noticed he was young, around twenty-five, and he had a serious voice and a serious face.

"I'm sorry I can't buy any," I said to him. "I haven't any money."

"You got fifty cents," he answered. "That's all they cost—five stars for fifty cents. Don't you want to help the war wounded?"

"I would like to very much," I said, "but I haven't even carfare to ride home. I have to walk."

"You don't say," he said. "You haven't even got a dime, eh?"

"Not today," I said. "I'll have some money tomorrow,

and if I should see you then I'll be glad to buy your silver stars."

I noticed that we were walking together. He had put the cover on the box he was carrying.

"I wouldn't let you buy these tin stars tomorrow if I met you," he suddenly spoke up.

"Why not?" I asked.

"Because they're fakes," he said. "The money doesn't go to any war wounded. Half of what I get I keep. The other half goes to a couple crooks I'm working for. Where you going?"

"I was going to one of those meetings on the corner," I said.

"There's one a couple blocks down," he said. "I just worked the crowd there. I got three bucks."

I didn't say anything.

"I'm really a war veteran myself," he went on. "There's no fake about that. I was in France and Germany. Infantry. The reason I'm working for these crooks now selling these fake stars is I don't want to go home. My pa wants me, but I don't want to go."

"Why don't you?" I asked.

"Because he wants me to work on his farm," he said. "He's got a farm in Ohio. I said to him, nothing doing. I'm not going to be a lousy farmer and work all my life for nothing like you. We had a fight, and I lit out. I was on the bum a while and couldn't connect with a job. Then I run into this outfit with the fake stars. They bought me a couple drinks, and I agreed to go in with them. It's easy money."

He didn't say anything for a while. Then he stopped walking.

"Can you stand here awhile?" he said. "I want to ask you something."

I stood in front of a grocery store. He smiled at me for the first time.

"What I want to ask you," he said, "is if you'll marry me."

I didn't answer him.

"I mean it," he got excited. "If you'll marry me, I'll go back to the farm with you. And I'll be a farmer. It wouldn't be so bad. We could have fun. There's a town twenty miles away. What do you say?"

"You don't even know who I am or what I am," I said.

"I like your looks," he said. "I've seen a lot of girls. There's something about you I like. It's different."

"You shouldn't ask a strange girl to marry you," I said. "You're liable to get into trouble."

"What trouble?" he asked.

"What if she were somebody no good, some criminal or something?" I said.

He looked at me for a while and then answered.

"You're no criminal or 'something.' I'm willing to take a chance. I got enough money for train fare back to the farm. Come on, what do you say—will you marry me?"

I shook my head because I could hardly talk. My heart hurt me. There was something so lonely about this young man who had been a soldier and who was selling fake tin stars that I wanted to cry.

I squeezed his arm and said, "I can't marry you," and walked away quickly. He didn't follow me.

When I looked back he had taken the cover off his box of tin stars and was moving toward a crowd near a street corner.

8

I BEGIN
A NEW DREAM

Yोu sit alone. It's night outside. Automobiles roll down Sunset Boulevard like an endless string of beetles. Their rubber tires make a purring high-class noise. You're hungry, and you say, "It's good for my waistline not to eat. There's nothing finer than a washboard belly."

And you say your speech lesson out loud:

"Ariadne arose from her couch in the snows in the Akrakaronian mountains." Followed by "Hail to thee, blithe spirit, bird thou never wert."

The lessons are a dollar apiece. For a dollar you could buy a pair of stockings and a hamburger sandwich. But stockings and a hamburger will never make you an actress. Speech lessons may. So with bare legs and empty stomach you hit the consonants of "Hail to thee, blithe spirit."

I used to think as I looked out on the Hollywood night, "There must be thousands of girls sitting alone like me dreaming of becoming a movie star. But I'm not going to worry about them. I'm dreaming the hardest."

You don't have to know anything to dream hard. I knew nothing about acting. I had never read a book about it, or tried to do it, or discussed it with anyone. I was ashamed to tell the few people I knew of what I was dreaming. I said I was hoping to make a living as a model. I called on all the model agencies and found a job now and then.

But there was this secret in me—acting. It was like being in jail and looking at a door that said "This Way Out."

Acting was something golden and beautiful. It was like the bright colors Norma Jean used to see in her daydreams. It wasn't an art. It was like a game you played that enabled you to step out of the dull world you knew into worlds so bright they made your heart leap just to think of them.

When I was eight I used to look out of the orphan asylum window at night and see a big lighted-up sign that read "R.K.O. Radio Pictures." I hated the sign. It reminded me of the smell of glue. My mother had once taken me to the studio where she worked. The smell of the wet film she cut and spliced had stuck in my nose.

That was Norma Jean's nose. Norma Dougherty, the aspiring actress, had no such feelings toward studio signs. To her they were the beacons of a Promised Land—the land of Ingrid Bergman, Claudette Colbert, Joan Crawford, Bette Davis, Olivia de Haviland, Gene Tierney, Jennifer Jones.

That's the way it was when I sat alone in my Hollywood room. I went to sleep hungry and woke up hungry. And I thought all actors and actresses were geniuses sitting on the front porch of Paradise—the movies.

9

HIGHER, HIGHER,
HIGHER

I'VE NEVER read anything about the Hollywood I knew in those first years. No hint of it is ever in the movie fan magazines. If there are any books on the subject, I must have skipped them, along with the few million other books I haven't read.

The Hollywood I knew was the Hollywood of failure. Nearly everybody I met suffered from malnutrition or suicide impulses. It was like the line in the poem, "Water, water everywhere but not a drop to drink." Fame, fame everywhere but not a hello for us.

We ate at drugstore counters. We sat in waiting rooms. We were the prettiest tribe of panhandlers that ever overran a town. And there were so many of us! Beauty contest winners, flashy college girls, home grown sirens from every state in the union. From cities and farms. From factories, vaudeville circuits, dramatic schools, and one from an orphan asylum.

And around us were the wolves. Not the big wolves inside the studio gates, but the little ones—talent agents without offices, press agents without clients, contact men without contacts, and managers. The drugstores and cheap cafés were full of managers ready to put you over if you enrolled under their banner. Their banner was usually a bed sheet.

I met them all. Phoniness and failure were all over them. Some were vicious and crooked. But they were as near to the movies as you could get. So you sat with them, listening to their lies and schemes. And you saw Hollywood with their eyes—an overcrowded brothel, a merry-go-round with beds for horses.

Among the phonies and failures were also a set of has-beens. These were mostly actors and actresses who had been dropped by the movies—nobody knew why, least of all themselves. They had played "big parts." They had scrapbooks full of "stills" and write-ups. And they were full of anecdotes about the big bosses with the magic names who ran the studios—Goldwyn, Zanuck, Mayer, Selznick, Schenck, Warner, Cohn. They had rubbed shoulders with them and exchanged conversations with them. Sitting in the cheap café nursing a glass of beer for an hour, they talked about the great ones, calling them by their first names. "Sam said to me," and "I told L.B.," and "I'll never forget Darryl's excitement when he saw the rushes."

When I remember this desperate, lie-telling, dime-hunting Hollywood I knew only a few years ago I get a little homesick. It was a more human place than the paradise I dreamed of and found. The people in it, the phonies and failures, were more colorful than the great men and successful artists I was to know soon.

Even the crooks who threw me curves and set traps for me seem pleasant, mellow characters. There was Harry, the photographer, who kept photographing me when he had enough money to buy plates for his view camera.

"I know a real hot agent," said Harry, "who's crazy about you. He saw one of your stills and blew his top. And he's no alley runner. He used to be a big man in Budapest."

"What kind of a big man, Harry?"

"A producer. You've heard of Reinhardt?"

"Oh, yes."

"Well, he was next in line to Reinhardt," said Harry. "You'll like him. He thinks big."

The three of us sat in a cheap café the next evening. The proprietor knew better than to send the waiter over to see if we wanted anything. Harry and I had been there before. The third at our table, Mr. Lazlo, didn't look any more promising as a customer. Mr. Lazlo was fat, unshaved, bald-headed, bleary-eyed, and his shirt collar was a little frayed. But he was a fine conversationalist. He spoke with a fascinating accent. It was hard to imagine that so cultured a man could be a bum. But I knew he was, or what would he be doing with Harry and me?

"So you have ambition to be a great actress," said Mr. Lazlo.

I nodded.

"Wonderful," said Mr. Lazlo. "How would you like not only to be a big star but also to own your own movie studio and make only the finest movies. No Hollywood junk. But art—real art."

"I'd like that," I said.

"Good," said Mr. Lazlo. "Now I know where you stand."

"Wait till you hear his ideas," said Harry. "I told you he thinks big."

"In Budapest," said Mr. Lazlo, "if I wanted a few hundred thousand dollars I have only to telephone the bank, and they send over a wagon with the money." He patted my hand. "You are very beautiful. I would like to buy you the kind of dinner I used to have every night—in Budapest."

"I've already eaten," I said.

"You are lucky," Mr. Lazlo sighed. "But first, before I go on—you are definitely interested in the project, may I ask?"

"I haven't heard it yet."

"Are you willing to become a wife?" Mr. Lazlo asked.

"Whose?" I asked back.

"The wife of a millionaire," said Mr. Lazlo. "He has authorized me to ask you this question."

"Does he know me?"

"He has studied your photographs," said Mr. Lazlo. "And he has picked you out from fifty other girls."

"I didn't know I was in any contest," I said.

"No cracks," said Harry. "This is high finance."

"The gentleman who wishes to marry you," said Mr. Lazlo, "is seventy-one years of age. He has high blood pressure—and no living relatives. He is alone in the world."

"He doesn't sound very enticing," I said.

"My dear child," Mr. Lazlo took my hand. His own was trembling with excitement. "You will inherit everything in six months. Maybe less."

"You mean he'll die if I marry him?" I asked.

"I guarantee it," said Mr. Lazlo.

"That's like murder," I said to Harry.

"In six months you will be a widow with two million dollars," said Mr. Lazlo. "You will keep the first million. Harry and I will split equally the second."

I lay in bed unable to sleep that night. I would never marry or even see Mr. Lazlo's dying millionaire, but it was exciting to think about it. I went around for a week imagining myself living in a castle on a hill—with a swimming pool and a hundred bathing suits.

Mr. Lazlo was one of the nicer of the scheme peddlers I met. There were a dozen not nearly as nice. Of these Mr. Sylvester was one.

My phone rang in my room.

"This is John Sylvester speaking," the voice said. "You don't know me but I'm a talent scout for Mr. Samuel Goldwyn."

I managed to say, "How do you do."

"We're looking for a girl of your general appearance," said Mr. Sylvester, "for one of the parts in the new Goldwyn picture. It's not a big part, but a very important one."

"Do you want to see me now?" I asked.

"Yes, I'll pick you up in a few minutes," Mr. Sylvester said. "I'm in the vicinity. And we'll go over to the studio."

"I'll be downstairs," I said.

I stood in front of my house and shook with excitement. It had happened! I wouldn't fail! Once they let me inside nothing would ever get me out. An important part! In a Goldwyn picture! He made the best ones. And he made stars, too.

A car stopped, and a middle-aged man smiled at me.

"Hop in, Miss Dougherty," he said.

I hopped in. We drove to the rear gate of the Goldwyn Studio.

"I always go in this way," Mr. Sylvester said. "It's a short cut."

It was seven o'clock and the place was deserted.

"We'll go to my office," Mr. Sylvester said, steering me by the elbow. "I'll audition you there."

We walked up a flight of steps, down a hallway. Mr. Sylvester stopped in front of a door.

"I hope they haven't locked me out," he said. "No—still open."

I noticed the name Dugan on the door and Mr. Sylvester said, patting my back, "Dugan and I share this office—for audition purposes."

It was a well-furnished office. Mr. Sylvester told me to sit down on the couch.

"What do you want me to audition?" I asked.

Mr. Sylvester picked a script from the desk and handed it to me. It was the first movie script I had ever held in my hands.

"Which part do you wish me to read?" I asked. I could hardly get the words out of my mouth. I kept thinking, "Get hold of yourself. You're an actress. You mustn't let your face twitch."

"Try one of the long speeches," Mr. Sylvester said.

I looked up at him surprised. He seemed almost as excited as me. I opened the script and began to read.

"Would you please raise your dress a few inches," Mr. Sylvester interrupted.

I lifted the hem above my knee and kept on reading.

"A little higher please," said Mr. Sylvester.

I lifted the hem to my thighs without missing a word of the speech.

"I will always love you." I read in the throbbing voice I used for "Hail To Thee, Blithe Spirit," "No matter what becomes of me, Alfred."

"A little higher," Mr. Sylvester said again.

I thought that Mr. Sylvester was probably in a hurry and wanted to audition my figure and emotional talents at the same time. Still reciting from the script I pulled my dress up and uncovered my thighs. And suddenly Mr. Sylvester was on the couch. For a moment I was too sick at heart to move. I saw Mr. Sylvester plain. The whole thing was a fake. He didn't work for Goldwyn. It wasn't his office. He had pulled the audition gag in order to get me alone on a couch. I sat with my dress up and the treasured script in my hand while Mr. Sylvester started pawing me. Then I moved. I socked him in the eye, jumped up, kicked him, and banged my heel down on his toes—and ran out of the building.

For some time afterward Mr. Sylvester's words haunted me as if I had heard the true voice of Hollywood—"Higher, higher, higher."

I GET THROUGH
THE LOOKING
GLASS

IN HOLLYWOOD a girl's virtue is much less important than her hair-do. You're judged by how you look, not by what you are. Hollywood's a place where they'll pay you a thousand dollars for a kiss, and fifty cents for your soul. I know, because I turned down the first offer often enough and held out for the fifty cents.

It wasn't because I had moral ideas. Nor because I saw what happened to girls who took money from men and let men support them as their sweeties. Nothing happened to such girls that wouldn't have happened to them anyway. Sometimes they got ditched and had to hook up with new lovers; or they got their names in the movie columns for being seen in the smart places, and this landed them jobs in the studios. Or, after going from love nest to love nest for a few years, they met someone who fell in love with them and got married and had children. A few of them even became famous.

It may be different in other places, but in Hollywood "being virtuous" is a juvenile sounding phrase like "having the mumps."

Maybe it was the nickel Mr. Kimmel once gave me, or maybe it was the five dollars a week the orphanage used to sell me for, but men who tried to buy me with money made me sick. There were plenty of them. The mere fact that I turned down offers ran my price up.

I was young, blonde, and curvaceous, and I had learned to talk huskily like Marlene Dietrich and to walk a little wantonly and to bring emotion into my eyes when I wanted to. And though these achievements landed me no job they brought a lot of wolves whistling at my heels. They weren't just little wolves with big schemes and frayed cuffs. There were bona fide check signers, also.

I rode with them in their limousines and sat in swanky cafés with them, where I usually ate like a horse to make up for a week of skimpy drugstore counter meals.

And I went to the big Beverly Hills homes with them and sat by while they played gin or poker. I was never at ease in these homes or in the swanky cafés. For one thing my clothes became cheap and shabby looking in swell surroundings. I had to sit with my legs in such a position that the runs or the mends in my stockings wouldn't show. And I had to keep my elbows out of sight for the same reason.

The men like to show off to each other and to the kibitzers by gambling for high stakes. When I saw them hand hundred and even thousand dollar bills to each other, I felt something bitter in my heart. I remembered how much twenty-five cents and even nickels meant to the people I had known, how happy ten dollars would have made them, how a hundred dollars would have changed their whole lives.

When the men laughed and pocketed the thousands of dollars of winnings as if they were made of tissue paper, I remembered my Aunt Grace and me waiting in line at the Holmes Bakery to buy a sackful of stale bread for a quarter to live on a whole week. And I remembered how she had gone with one of her lenses missing from her glasses for three months because she couldn't afford the fifty cents to buy its replacement. I remembered all the sounds and smells of poverty, the fright in people's eyes when they lost jobs, and the way they skimped and drudged in order to get through the week. And I saw the blue dress and white blouse walking the two miles to school again, rain or shine, because a nickel was too big a sum to raise for bus fare.

I didn't dislike the men for being rich or being indifferent to money. But something hurt me in my heart when I saw their easy come, easy go thousand dollar bills.

One evening a rich man said to me, "I'll buy you a

couple of real outfits, fur coats and all. And I'll pay your rent in a nice apartment and give you an eating allowance. And you don't even have to go to bed with me. All I ask is to take you out to cafés and parties and for you to act as if you were my girl. And I'll say good night to you outside your door and never ask you to let me in. It'll just be a make-believe affair. What do you say?"

I answered him, "I don't like men with fancy schemes like you. I like straightforward wolves better. I know how to get along with them. But I'm always nervous with liars."

"What makes you think I'm lying?" he asked.

"Because if you didn't want me you wouldn't try to buy me," I said.

I didn't take their money, and they couldn't get by my front door, but I kept riding in their limousines and sitting beside them in the swanky places. There was always a chance a job and not another wolf might spot you. Besides, there was the matter of food. I never felt squeamish about eating my head off. Food wasn't part of any purchase price.

Y CHIEF problem next to eating, stockings, and rent, was my automobile. I had made a down payment on a small, secondhand car. But the hundred and fifty I still owed on it was Sweepstake money.

The second month I received a letter saying if I didn't make the fifty dollar monthly payment the company would have to repossess the car. I inquired of a girl I knew at Central Casting what the word meant and she told me.

The third month a man knocked on my door, showed me a document, and repossessed my car.

"On the receipt of fifty dollars," the man said, "the company will be glad to restore the car to your custody."

A movie job hunter without a car in Hollywood was like a fireman without a fire engine. There were at least a dozen studios and agents' offices you had to visit every day. And they were in a dozen different districts, miles away from each other.

Nothing came of these visits. You sat in a waiting room of the Casting Department. An assistant came out of a door, looked over the assembled group and said, "There's nothing today. Leave your names and phone numbers." That was almost a break—the second sentence. "Leave your names and phone numbers." Usually they uttered only the first sentence.

In the Agency office it was a little more complicated. Because the agents weren't as sincere as the Casting Departments. They were inclined to string you along, utter a few wolf calls, make promises, and try out a wrestling hold or two. Nothing came of it, but you had to keep coming back. Agents sometimes had "ins" and jobs.

Ring Lardner wrote a story once about a couple of girls who saved up their money and went to Palm Beach, Florida, to mingle with the social elite of that famous resort. He said they stopped at a swell hotel, and every evening "They romped out on the veranda to enjoy a few snubs." That's the way it was with me. Except without an automobile, I could do very little romping.

I did everything possible to get the car back. I spent days tracking down the Marshall and the Sheriff of Los Angeles. I visited the company that had done the repossessing. I even contemplated calling up a few millionaires I knew. But I couldn't. When I started to dial one of their numbers a hot angry feeling filled me, and I had to hang up. I realized this wasn't quite normal, but all I could do was throw myself on the bed and start crying. I would cry and yell and beat the wall with my fists as if I were trying to break out of someplace. Then I would lie still for a day or two and go without food and wish I were dead—as if I were Norma Jean again looking out of the orphanage window.

The phone rang. It was a photographer I knew named Tom Kelley. He and his wife Natalie had been nice to me. I had posed for some beer ads for Tom.

"Come on over," he said. "I've got a job for you."

"This is a little different than the other jobs," Tom said when I got to his place. "But there's fifty dollars in it for you, if you want to do it."

I told Tom and Natalie about the repossessing of my car.

"For fifty dollars, I am ready to jump off a roof," I said.

"These pictures are for a calendar," said Tom, "and they will have to be in the nude."

"You mean completely nude?" I asked.

"That's it," said Tom, "except they will not be vulgar. You're ideal for the job not only because you have a fine shape but you're unknown. Nobody'll recognize you."

"I'm sure unknown," I said.

"It would be different if you were a starlet or some such thing," said Natalie. "Then somebody might recognize you on the calendar."

"With you there'll be no such trouble possible," said Tom. "It'll just be a picture of a beautiful nobody."

I spent the afternoon posing. I was a little confused at first, and something kept nudging me in my head. Sitting naked in front of a camera and striking joyous poses reminded me of the dreams I used to have as a child. I felt sad that this should be the only dream I ever had to come true.

After a few poses the depression left me. I liked my body. I was glad I hadn't eaten much in the past few days. The pictures would show a real washboard stomach. And what difference would it make—the nude of a "beautiful nobody?"

People have curious attitudes about nudity, just as they have about sex. Nudity and sex are the most commonplace things in the world. Yet people often act as if they were things that existed only on Mars. I thought of such matters as I posed, but the nudging continued in my head. What if I became an actress sometime? A great star? And somebody saw me on the calendar, and recognized me?

"What are you looking so serious about?" Tom asked.

"I was just thinking something," I said.

"What?"

"Nothing worth repeating," I said. "I'm just crazy. I get all kinds of crazy thoughts."

I had my car back the next day and was able to romp around from studio to studio and enjoy the usual quota of snubs.

I RUSHED to Aunt Grace with the big news. I had a job. I could enter a studio without being asked fifty questions. And I didn't have to sit in a waiting room. I was on a payroll as an actress.

"It's the finest studio in the world," I said. "20th Century-Fox."

Aunt Grace beamed and went to the stove for coffee.

"The people are all wonderful," I said, "and I'm going to be in a movie. It'll be a small part. But once I'm on the screen—"

I stopped and looked at Aunt Grace. She was still smiling at me. But she was standing still. Her face was pale, and she looked tired—as if life was something too heavy to carry much further.

I put my arms around her and helped her to the table.

"I'm all right," she said. "The coffee will fix me up fine."

"It'll be different now for all of us," I said. "I'll work hard."

We sat a long time and discussed a new name for me. The casting director had suggested I think up some more glamorous name than Norma Dougherty.

"I'd like to oblige him," I said. "Especially since Dougherty isn't my name anymore anyway."

"Haven't you any ideas for a name?" Aunt Grace asked.

I didn't answer. I had a name, a real name that thrilled me whenever I thought of it. It belonged to the man with the slouch hat and the Gable mustache. His photograph was now in my possession.

I tried the name out in my mind, but kept silent. My aunt was smiling at me. I felt she knew what I was thinking.

"The man at the studio suggested Marilyn," I said.

"That's a nice name," my Aunt said, "and it fits with your mother's maiden name."

I didn't know what that was.

"She was a Monroe," said Aunt Grace. "Her family goes way back. I have some papers and letters I'm keeping for your mother. They show that she was related to President Monroe of the United States."

"You mean I'm related to a president of the United States?" I asked.

"Directly descended," said Aunt Grace.

"It's a wonderful name," I said. "Marilyn Monroe. But I won't tell them about the president." I kissed Aunt Grace and said, "I'll try to make good on my own."

The assistant director said, "Now just walk up to Miss June Haver, smile at her, say hello, wave your right hand, and walk on. Got that?"

The bells rang. A hush fell over the set. The assistant director called, "Action!" I walked, smiled, waved my right hand and spoke. I was in the movies! I was one of those hundred to one shots—a "bit player."

There were a dozen of us on the set, bit players, with a gesture to make and a line or two to recite. Some of them were veteran bit players. After ten years in the movies they were still saying one line and walking ten feet toward nowhere. A few were young and had nice bosoms. But I knew they were different from me. They didn't have my illusions. My illusions didn't have anything to do with being a fine actress. I knew how third rate I was. I could actually feel my lack of talent, as if it were cheap clothes I was wearing inside. But, my God, how I wanted to learn! To change, to improve! I didn't want anything else. Not men, not money, not love, but the ability to act. With the arc lights on me and the camera pointed at me, I suddenly knew myself. How clumsy, empty, uncultured I was! A sullen orphan with a goose egg for a head.

But I would change. I stood silent and staring. Men were

smiling at me and trying to catch my eye. Not the actors or the director and his assistants. They were important people and important people try to catch the eye only of other important people. But the grips and electricians and the other healthy looking workmen had grinning friendly faces for me. I didn't return their grins. I was too busy being desperate. I had a new name, Marilyn Monroe. I had to get born. And this time better than before.

My bit was cut out of the picture *Scudda Hoo, Scudda Hay.* I didn't mind when I heard about it. I would be better in the next picture. I'd been hired for six months. In six months I'd show them.

I spent my salary on dramatic lessons, on dancing lessons, and singing lessons. I bought books to read. I sneaked scripts off the set and sat up alone in my room reading them out loud in front of the mirror. And an odd thing happened to me. I fell in love with myself—not how I was but how I was going to be.

I used to say to myself, what the devil have you got to be proud about, Marilyn Monroe? And I'd answer, "Everything, everything." And I'd walk slowly and turn my head slowly as if I were a queen.

One night another bit player, a male, invited me out for dinner.

"I haven't any money," I warned him. "Have you?"

"No," he said. "But I've received a sort of invitation to a party. And I would like to take you along. All the stars will be there."

We arrived at the Beverly Hills home at nine o'clock. It was a famous agent's house. I felt as frightened entering it as if I were breaking into a bank. My stockings had a few mends in them. I was wearing a ten dollar dress. And my shoes! I prayed nobody would look at my shoes. I said to myself, now's the time to feel like a queen, you dope—not when you're alone in the room with nobody looking. But the queen feeling wouldn't come. The best I could manage was to walk stiff legged into a large hall and stand staring like a frozen blonde at dinner jackets and evening gowns.

My escort whispered to me, "The food's in the other room. Come on." He went off without me. I remained in the hall, looking into a room full of wonderful furniture and wonderful people. Jennifer Jones was sitting on a couch. Olivia de Haviland was standing near a little table. Gene Tierney was laughing next to her. There were so many others I couldn't focus on them. Evening gowns and famous faces drifted around in the room laughing and chatting. Diamonds glittered. There were men, too, but I only looked at one. Clark Gable stood by himself holding a highball and smiling wistfully at the air. He looked so familiar that it made me dizzy.

I stood as straight as I could and put on the highest class expression I knew. But I couldn't enter the room where the laughter and diamonds were.

A voice spoke.

"My dear young lady," it said. "Do come and sit by my side."

It was a charming voice, a little fuzzy with liquor, but very distinguished. I turned and saw a man sitting by himself on the stairway. He was holding a drink in his hand. His face was sardonic like his voice.

"Do you mean me?" I asked.

"Yes," he said. "Pardon me if I don't rise. My name is George Sanders."

I said, "How do you do."

"I presume you also have a name," he scowled at me.

"I'm Marilyn Monroe," I said.

"You will forgive me for not having heard it before," said Mr. Sanders. "Do sit down—beside me."

"May I have the honor of asking you to marry me?" he said solemnly. "The name, in case you have forgotten, is Sanders."

I smiled at him and didn't answer.

"You are naturally a little reluctant to marry one who is not only a stranger, but an actor," Mr. Sanders said. "I can understand your hesitancy—particularly on the second ground. An actor is not quite a human being—but then, who is?"

Mr. Sanders' handsome and witty face suddenly looked at me, intently.

"Blonde," he said, "pneumatic, and full of peasant health. Just the type meant for me."

I thought he was going to put his arm around me but he didn't. His voice sounded sleepy as he continued.

"Please think it over, Miss Monroe. I can promise you only one thing if you marry me. You'll become one of the most glamorous stars in Hollywood. I'll help you. Word of honor."

Mr. Sanders put his glass down and dozed off.

I left him on the stairs and walked across the hall, out of the mansion door into the Beverly Hills night. I felt grateful to Mr. Sanders for having spoken to me. But out of the incident came my first Hollywood feud.

I'll skip ahead and tell the feud story here. A year and a half later I was still broke and looking for jobs, but the first little buzz of success had touched my name. I'd been on the screen in *The Asphalt Jungle,* and audiences had whistled at me—just as the wolves on the beach had done the first time I'd worn a bathing suit. And though I didn't seem able to land another job after my "great success," the photographers were after me as a model.

Among these was Tony Beauchamp who was one of the more important camera artists in Hollywood. He was married to Sarah Churchill. I had been to his studio often to sit for pictures. One day he asked me to come to his home on Sunday afternoon "for cocktails."

I was thrilled by the invitation and eager to meet his wife. I had always looked up to Winston Churchill as an oldish but very noble man.

The Beauchamp home was on the beach. I drove out alone dressed in a sweater and skirt. I hadn't yet learned that "come for cocktails" meant a party. I thought the cocktails would be only for Mr. and Mrs. Beauchamp and me.

When I entered the Beauchamp home I stood still and didn't move. It was filled with people all drinking cocktails. The only person I knew was Tony Beauchamp.

"Make yourself at home," he said and introduced me to his wife. I said how do you do and remained standing still. The Beauchamps moved on.

I noticed a commotion among the guests at the other end of the crowded room. A blonde with a funny accent was cutting loose about something. I couldn't make out her words, but she was whooping away in unmistakable fury. I saw her take a tall man by the arm and march him out of the room. The tall man looked familiar.

Tony came up to me with a grin.

"Dear, dear," he said, "what have you done to Zsa Zsa Gabor?"

"Who is that?" I asked.

"The Hungarian bombshell," said Tony. "You just drove her out of the party fuming!"

"Maybe she didn't approve of my sweater," I said. "I wouldn't have worn it if I'd known it was a party."

"Oh no," said Tony. "It's deeper than that. Zsa Zsa said Sarah and I couldn't expect nice people to remain at our party if people like you joined it. Now, frankly, Marilyn—what in heaven's name did you do to her?"

"Nothing," I said. "I never even saw her before."

I walked over to have a look at this Hungarian bombshell. I saw she was one of those blondes who put on ten years if you take a close look at them. I also saw that the tall, handsome man she was clucking and making other Hungarian chicken noises at was George Sanders. I learned from Tony beside me that Mr. Sanders was her husband.

Poor Mr. Sanders, he had made that stairway speech once too often.

13

I DIDN'T LIKE PARTIES
BUT I LIKED
MR. SCHENCK

I WAS TO go to a number of fancy Hollywood parties and stand among the glamorous figures dressed as well as any of them and laugh as if I were overcome with joy, but I never felt any more at ease than I did the first time I watched from the hallway.

The chief fun people get out of those parties comes the next day when they are able to spread the news of the famous people with whom they associated at So-and-So's house. Most parties are run on the star system. In Hollywood a star isn't only an actor or actress or movie executive. It can also be somebody who has recently been arrested for something, or beaten up or exposed in a love triangle. If it was played up in the newspapers then this person is treated as a social star as long as his or her publicity continues.

I don't know if high society is different in other cities, but in Hollywood important people can't stand to be invited someplace that isn't full of other important people. They don't mind a few unfamous people being present because they make good listeners. But if a star or a studio chief or any other great movie personages find themselves sitting among a lot of nobodies, they get frightened as if somebody was trying to demote them.

I could never understand why important people are always so eager to dress up and come together to look at each other. Maybe three or four of them will have something to say to somebody, but the twenty or thirty others will just sit around like lumps on a log and stare at each other with false smiles. The host usually bustles about trying to get the guests involved in some kind of a game or guessing contest. Or he tries to get somebody to make a speech about something so as to start a general argument. But usually the guests fail to respond, and the party just drags on with nothing happening till the Sandman arrives. This is the signal for the guests to start leaving. Nearly everybody draws the line at falling asleep outright at a party.

The reason I went to parties of this sort was to advertise myself. There was always the possibility that someone might insult me or make a pass at me, which would be good publicity if it got into the movie columns. But even if nothing extra happened, just to be reported in the movie columns as having been present at a movie society gathering is very good publicity. Sometimes it is the only favorable mention the movie queens can get. There was also the consideration that if my studio bosses saw me standing among the regular movie stars they might get to thinking of me as a star also.

Going out socially in this fashion was the hardest part of my campaign to make good. But after a few months, I learned how to reduce the boredom considerably. This was to arrive around two hours late at a party. You not only make a special entrance, which was good advertising, but nearly everybody was likely to be drunk by that time. Important people are much more interesting when they are drunk and seem much more like human beings.

There is another side of a Hollywood party that is very important socially. It is a place where romances are made and unmade. Nearly everybody who attends an important party not only hopes to get favorably mentioned in the movie columns but also to fall in love or get started on a new seduction before the evening is over. It is hard to explain how you can fall in love while you are being bored to death, but I know it's true, because it happened to me several times.

As soon as I could afford an evening gown, I bought the loudest one I could find. It was a bright red low cut dress, and my arrival in it usually infuriated half the women present. I was sorry in a way to do this, but I had a long way to go, and I needed a lot of advertising to get there.

The first fame I achieved was a wave of gossip that identified me as Joe Schenck's girl. Mr. Schenck had invited me to his Beverly Hills mansion for dinner one evening. Then he fell into the habit of inviting me two or three times a week.

I went to Mr. Schenck's mansion the first few times because he was one of the heads of my studio. After that I went because I liked him. Also the food was very good, and there were always important people at the table. These weren't party figures but were Mr. Schenck's personal friends.

I seldom spoke three words during dinner but would sit at Mr. Schenck's elbow and listen like a sponge. The fact that people began to talk about me being Joe Schenck's girl didn't annoy me at first. But later it did annoy me. Mr. Schenck never so much as laid a finger on my wrist, or tried to. He was interested in me because I was a good table ornament and because I was what he called an "offbeat" personality.

I liked sitting around the fireplace with Mr. Schenck and hearing him talk about love and sex. He was full of wisdom on these subjects, like some great explorer. I also liked to look at his face. It was as much the face of a town as of a man. The whole history of Hollywood was in it.

Perhaps the chief reason I was happy to have won Mr. Schenck's friendship was the great feeling of security it gave me. As a friend and protégée of one of the heads of my own studio, what could go wrong for me?

I got the answer to that question one Monday morning. I was called into the casting department and informed that I was being dropped by the studio and that my presence would no longer be required. I couldn't talk. I sat listening and unable to move.

The casting official explained that I had been given several chances and that while I had acquitted myself fairly well it was the opinion of the studio that I was not photogenic. That was the reason, he said, that Mr. Zanuck had had me cut out of the pictures in which I had played bit parts.

"Mr. Zanuck feels that you may turn into an actress sometime," said the official, "but that your type of looks is definitely against you."

I went to my room and lay down in bed and cried. I cried for a week. I didn't eat or talk or comb my hair. I kept crying as if I were at a funeral burying Marilyn Monroe.

It wasn't only that I'd been fired. If they had dropped me because I couldn't act it would have been bad enough. But it wouldn't have been fatal. I could learn, improve, and become an actress. But how could I ever change my looks? And I'd thought that was the part of me that couldn't miss!

And imagine how wrong my looks must be if even Mr. Schenck had to agree to fire me. I lay crying day after day. I hated myself for having been such a fool and had illusions about how attractive I was. I got out of bed and looked in the mirror. Something horrible had happened. I wasn't attractive. I saw a coarse, crude-looking blonde. I was looking at myself with Mr. Zanuck's eyes. And I saw what he had seen—a girl whose looks were too big a handicap for a career in the movies.

The phone rang. Mr. Schenck's secretary invited me to dinner. I went. I sat through the evening feeling too ashamed to look into anyone's eyes. That's the way you feel when you're beaten inside. You don't feel angry at those who've beaten you. You just feel ashamed. I had tasted this shame early—when a family would kick me out and send me back to the orphanage.

When we were sitting in the living room Mr. Schenck said to me, "How are things going at the studio?"

I smiled at him because I was glad he hadn't had a hand in my being fired.

"I lost my job there last week," I said.

Mr. Schenck looked at me and I saw a thousand stories in his face—stories of all the girls he had known who had lost jobs, of all the actresses he had heard boasting and giggling with success and then moaning and sobbing with defeat. He didn't try to console me. He didn't take my hand or make any promises. The history of Hollywood looked out of his tired eyes at me and he said, "Keep going."

"I will," I said.

"Try X Studio," Mr. Schenck said. "There might be something there."

When I was leaving Mr. Schenck's house I said to him, "I'd like to ask you a personal question. Do I look any different to you than I used to?"

"You look the same as always," said Mr. Schenck, "only get some sleep and quit crying."

"Thank you," I said.

I called X Studio two days later. The casting department was very polite. Yes, they had a place for me. They would put me on the payroll and see that I was given a chance at any part that came up. Mr. A., the casting director, smiled, squeezed my hand and added, "You ought to go a long way here. I'll watch out for a good part for you."

I returned to my room at the Studio Club feeling alive again. And the daydreams started coming back—kind of on tiptoe. The casting director saw hundreds of girls every week, whom he turned down, real actresses and beauties of every sort. There must be something special about me for him to have hired me right off, after a first look.

There was something special about me in the casting director's eyes, but I didn't find it out till much later. Mr. Schenck had called up the head of X Studio and asked him as a favor to give me a job.

I received several "extra girl" calls from the studio and worked in a few scenes as "background." Then one day Mr. A., the casting director, telephoned. He wanted me in his office at four o'clock. I spent the day bathing and fixing my hair and reciting out loud different parts I had learned. And giving myself instructions. This was the big chance. Mr. A. wouldn't have called me himself if it wasn't for a real part. But I mustn't act overeager, or start babbling, or grin with joy. I must sit quietly and have dignity every minute.

Mr. A. wasn't in his office, but his secretary smiled at me and told me to go inside and wait for him.

I sat straight in one of Mr. A's inner office chairs waiting and practicing dignity. A door at the back of the office opened, and a man came in. I had never met him, but I knew who he was. He was head of X Studio, and as great a man as Mr. Schenck or Mr. Zanuck.

"Hello, Miss Monroe," he said.

He came over to me, put his hand on my arm, and said, "Come on, we'll go in my office and talk."

"I don't think I can leave," I said. "I'm waiting for Mr. A. He telephoned me about a part."

"The hell with Mr. A.," said the great man. "He'll know where you are."

I hesitated, and he added, "What's the matter with you? You dopey or something? Don't you know I'm the boss around here?"

I followed him through the back door into an office three times larger than Mr. A's.

"Turn around," said the great man. I turned like a model.

"You look all right," he grinned. "Nicely put together."

I said, "Thank you."

"Sit down," he said, "I want to show you something."

The great man rummaged through his oversized desk. I looked at his office. The tables were full of bronze Oscars and silver cups and all sorts of other prizes he had won with his movies. I had never seen an office like this before—the office where the head of an entire studio presided. Here was where all the great stars, producers, and directors came for conferences, and where all the decisions were made by the great man behind his battleship of a desk.

"Hold all calls," the great man spoke into a box on the desk. He beamed at me. "Here's what I wanted to show you."

He brought a large photograph to my chair. It was a picture of a yacht.

"How do you like it?" he asked.

"It's very beautiful," I said.

"You're invited," he said. He put his hand on my neck.

"Thank you," I said. "I've never been to a party on a yacht."

"Who said anything about a party," the great man scowled at me. "I'm inviting you, nobody else. Do you want to come, or not?"

"I'll be glad to join you and your wife on your yacht, Mr. X.," I said.

The great man looked fiercely at me.

"Leave my wife out of this," he said. "There'll be nobody on the yacht except you and me. And some expensive sailors. We'll leave in an hour. And we'll take a cruise overnight. I have to be back tomorrow evening for my wife's dinner party. No way of getting out of it."

He stopped and scowled at me again.

"What's the idea of standing there and staring at me," he demanded, "like I had insulted you. I know who you are. You're Joe Schenck's girl. He called me up to do him a favor and give you a job. Is that a reason for you to get insulting?"

I smiled at the great man.

"I don't mean to be insulting, Mr. X," I said.

"Good," he was beaming again. "We'll have a fine cruise, and I can tell you now, you won't regret it."

He put his arms around me. I didn't move.

"I'm very grateful to you for the invitation, Mr. X," I said, "but I'm busy this week and so I shall have to refuse it."

His arm dropped from me. I started for the door. He stood still, and I felt I had to say something else. He was a great man, and he held my future in his hands. Seducing employees was just a normal routine for him. I mustn't act as if I thought he was some kind of monster, or he would never—

I turned in the doorway. Mr. X was standing glaring at me. I had never seen a man so angry. I made my voice as casual and friendly as I could.

"I hope you invite me some time again when I can accept your invitation," I said.

The great man pointed his finger at me.

"This is your last chance," he said fiercely.

I walked through the door and out of the office where movie stars were made.

"Maybe he's watching me," I thought. "I mustn't let him see me upset."

I drove to my room in my car. Yes, there was something special about me, and I knew what it was. I was the kind of girl they found dead in a hall bedroom with an empty bottle of sleeping pills in her hand.

14

THE POLICE
ENTER MY LIFE

B UT THINGS weren't entirely black—not yet. They really never are. When you're young and healthy you can plan on Monday to commit suicide, and by Wednesday you're laughing again.

After lying around for a few days feeling sorry for myself and feeling what a failure I was, something would come back into my heart again. I wouldn't say things out loud, but I could hear them as if voices were talking to me, get up, you haven't begun yet, you're different, something wonderful is going to happen.

And wonderful things did happen on the ocean bottom—in a small way.

I met kind people.

I had met a married couple who lived in Burbank in a small house. They said to me one evening while I was visiting them, "We're going away for a few months. Why don't you just live in our house while we're gone and save rent?"

I moved my suitcase and make up box to Burbank. I owned one suit, two plain dresses, two pairs of shoes, some darned stockings, a little lingerie, and a bathrobe. Moving wasn't hard.

It was around Christmas time, and I was worrying about where I would get money to buy a few Christmas presents with. It had been fun buying presents when I was on the studio payroll. I bought them chiefly for Aunt Grace or Aunt Anna.

When Aunt Grace was ill I would go shopping a whole day for her and buy a silk bed jacket, silk slippers, a fancy nightgown, and a bottle of perfume. I would put them all in one box and take it to her. Her happiness on seeing all the things in the box was worth a thousand times more than what they had cost.

This Christmas everything seemed extra gloomy. Not only had I flopped in my career, but there was a laziness in me that kept me from getting jobs. I preferred to lie around feeling sorry for myself and thinking how cruel and unfair the world was. As a result I didn't have any money. Even to eat, let alone to spend on presents.

Then one day I received word from the studio that I had forty dollars coming to me. I hurried over and collected it. The cashier handed me a check for the money. I was so excited I left the studio forgetting to cash it.

When I got off the bus in Hollywood Boulevard to do some shopping I didn't have a dime in my purse. I went into a drugstore and ate dinner, and then I offered to pay with the check. The manager refused to cash it, but he said he'd trust me if I'd give him my name and address. I did.

Then I went out and tried to cash the check in different places. Nobody would cash it.

I saw a policeman looking at me; so I went up to him.

"Pardon me, officer," I said. "Could you help me please? I want to get a check cashed, and I don't know where."

He smiled and said, "Well, that is a serious predicament. Come along, I'll see what I can do. What sort of a check is it?"

"It's a payroll check," I said, "from the 20th Century-Fox Studio."

"Are you employed there?" the policeman asked.

"I'm not employed there any longer," I said. "But they are still in business."

The policeman took me into a store. He spoke to the manager who agreed to cash the check.

"So you're an actress," said the policeman.

"I used to be," I said, "but, as I told you, I'm not working at the moment."

The manager brought the check back and said, "Would

you mind putting your name and address on the back of this?"

I did and noticed the policeman watching me write. I also looked at his face for the first time. He had dark hair and his eyes were close together.

After doing my shopping, I stopped in a doctor's office. I had a cold, and I had not slept for several nights. The doctor gave me a sleeping pill.

"I don't usually recommend sleeping pills," he said, "but you've been having hysterics too long. A good sleep will not only be good for your cold but cheer you up."

I went to bed early and took the pill. I'd been sleeping for a few hours when a noise woke me. I'd never heard this sort of noise before, but I knew what it was. Somebody was cutting the screen of the bedroom window.

I jumped out of bed and ran out of the house. I went around the side to look. A man was starting to climb into my bedroom window. I imitated a gruff male voice and called indignantly, "Hey, what are you doing there?"

The man pulled his head out of the window and looked toward me.

"Get away from here," I shouted again in a gruff voice, "or I'll call the police."

The man started toward me. I turned and ran like sixty.

It was around midnight. I ran down the deserted suburban street. I was barefooted, and I was wearing the new style of half nightgown. It came just a little below the waist.

I arrived at a neighbor's house and yelled. He came down with his wife behind him. She started yelling when she saw me. I explained about the man trying to break into my bedroom and asked the neighbor to go capture him.

The neighbor shook his head.

"The fellow probably has a gun," he said. "Burglars usually carry them."

"He's not a burglar," I said. "He was after me."

I telephoned the police and covered myself with a quilt.

The police took an hour to arrive. I went back to the house with them. They found the cut screen and footprints and everything.

"Well, you scared him off," the detective said. "You have nothing to worry about. You can go back to bed."

"But what if he returns?" I asked.

"Never happens," said the detective. "Once a burglar is scared off the premises he'll never return to that place. Just relax, miss, and go to sleep. We'll let you know if anything turns up."

There was a loud knocking on the door. I jumped two feet. It was around 1 A.M.

"Do you usually get company at this time of night?" the detective asked me.

"No," I said. "I never have any company. Nobody has ever come to call on me."

"Go open the door," the detective ordered.

I went to the door and opened it. It was the screen cutter. He made a grab for me, and I screamed.

The two detectives seized him.

"That's the man," I yelled. "He's the burglar!"

"What's all this?" the man scowled at the detectives holding him. "Marilyn's an old friend. Good old Marilyn." And he winked at me and said, "Tell 'em, honey."

"I don't know the man," I said. "He looks a little familiar, but I don't know him."

"Let me go," the man cried. "You can't arrest somebody for calling on an old friend."

"How about it?" one of the detectives said to me. "Let's have the truth, Miss Monroe. Is this an old sweetie of yours?"

I could feel that they were believing the man, and I was terrified they would go away and leave him alone with me.

"He's no burglar," the detective scowled at me. "He knows your name and address. He comes back after you chase him away. Obviously he's—"

The other detective was searching the man and pulled a revolver out of his pocket.

"Hey," he interrupted, "this is a police gun! Where'd you get this?"

At the words "police gun" I knew who the man was. It was the policeman with the eyes close together who had helped me cash my forty dollar check. He'd memorized the name and address as I wrote them on the back of the check.

I hadn't recognized him at first because he was out of uniform.

I told the detectives who he was. He denied it but they found a Los Angeles police card in his pocket.

They took him away.

The next day the detectives visited me. They told me the man was a new cop, that he was married and had a fourteen-month-old baby. They said they would rather I didn't file any charges against the man because it would give the police force a black eye.

"I don't want to punish him," I said, "but I would like to be sure he didn't try to do that to me again. Or to any other girl."

The detectives assured me he wouldn't. So I didn't file any charges. Instead I moved out.

I went back to a Hollywood bedroom, and I stayed in it for several days and nights without moving. I cried and stared out the window.

WHEN YOU'RE a failure in Hollywood—that's like starving to death outside a banquet hall with the smells of filet mignon driving you crazy. I lay in bed again day after day, not eating, not combing my hair. I kept remembering how I had sat in Mr. A's casting office controlling my excitement about the great luck that had finally come to me, and I felt like an idiot. There was going to be no luck in my life. The dark star I was born under was going to get darker and darker.

I cried and mumbled to myself. I'd go out and get a job as a waitress or clerk. Millions of girls were happy to work at jobs like that. Or I could work in a factory again. I wasn't afraid of any kind of work. I'd scrubbed floors and washed dishes ever since I could remember.

But there was something wouldn't let me go back to the world of Norma Jean. It wasn't ambition or a wish to be rich and famous. I didn't feel any pent up talent in me. I didn't even feel that I had looks or any sort of attractiveness. But there was a thing in me like a craziness that wouldn't let up. It kept speaking to me, not in words but in colors—scarlet and gold and shining white, greens and blues. They were the colors I used to dream about in my childhood when I had tried to hide from the dull, unloving world in which the orphanage slave, Norma Jean, existed.

I was still flying from that world, and it was still around me.

It was while I lay on this ocean bottom, figuring never to see daylight again, that I fell in love for the first time. I'd not only never been in love, but I hadn't ever dreamed of it. It was something that existed for other people—people who had families and homes.

But when I lay on this ocean bottom it hit me, hoisted me into the air, and stood me on my feet looking at the world as if I'd just been born.

He's married now to a movie star, and it might embarrass him if I used his real name, and her, too. I read in the paper that their marriage, only a year old, is heading for the Hollywood reefs where most of the movieland marriages come apart. A few years ago I might have felt like giving it a push, just for old times sake. But now I'm happy and I wish him well and I wish anybody he loves well.

I was coming out of the casting department at M.G.M. with the usual results—no job and no prospects—when a girl I knew introduced me to an ordinary looking man. All I could tell about him was that he wasn't an actor. Actors are often wonderful and charming people, but for a woman to love an actor is something like incest. It's like loving a brother with the same face and manners as your own.

We went to a café and sat down and talked. Or rather, he talked. I stared and listened. I was sick inside with failure, and there was no hope in me. His voice was like a medicine. He told me he was a musician and how much he liked to play the piano and why some music was better than other music. I didn't think of him as a man or a musician. All I thought was "He's alive and strong."

He called me up, and I always hurried to join him. The first thing I saw when I entered any place to meet him, no matter how crowded it was, was his face. It would jump out at me.

After a few weeks he knew I loved him. I hadn't said so, but I didn't have to. I stumbled when I went to sit down, my mouth hung open, my heart ached so much I wanted to cry all the time. If his hand touched mine by accident my knees buckled.

He smiled at me through all this as if I were half a joke. When he laughed at things I hadn't meant to be funny, I felt flattered. He talked a lot about women and the emptiness of their love. He had just been divorced and was very cynical. He had a six-year-old son whose custody had been granted him by the court.

One evening after he had put his son to bed he sat and played the piano for me. He played a long time. Then he did something that made my heart beat crazily. In order to see the music better he put on a pair of glasses. I had never seen him with glasses on.

I don't know why, but I had always been attracted to men who wore glasses. Now, when *he* put them on, I felt suddenly overwhelmed.

He stopped playing, removed his glasses and came over to me. He embraced and kissed me. My eyes closed, and a new life began for me.

I moved from the Studio Club where I was living to a place nearer his house so he could stop in on the way to work or home from work. I sat all day waiting for him. When I looked back on all the years I could remember, I shuddered. I knew now how cold and empty they had been. I had always thought of myself as someone unloved. Now I knew there had been something worse than that in my life. It had been my own unloving heart. I had loved myself a little, and Aunt Grace and Anna. How little it seemed now!

I sat alone thinking a lot about the past and understanding the frosty hearted child, Norma Jean. She would never have lived to grow up if her heart had had love in it. Now waiting for *him* when he was fifteen minutes late filled me with agony. Had I loved anyone or anything in my childhood and girlhood, what a thousand agonies there would have been every day! Maybe there were, and I had hidden them. Maybe that was why it hurt so now to love, and why my heart kept carrying on as if I were going to explode with pain and longing.

I thought a great deal about *him* and other men. My lover was a strong individual. I don't mean he was dominant. A strong man doesn't have to be dominant toward a woman. He doesn't match his strength against a woman weak with love for him. He matches it against the world.

When he came into my room and took me in his arms all my troubles were forgotten. I even forgot Norma Jean, and her eyes stopped looking out of mine. I even forgot about not being photogenic. A new me appeared in my skin—not an actress, not somebody looking for a world of bright colors. All the fame and color and genius I had dreamed of were in me. When he said "I love you" to me, it was better than a thousand critics calling me a great star.

I tried to figure out what was so different about my life than before *him*. It was the same—no hopes, no prospects, all doors closed. The troubles were still there, every one of them, but they were like dust swept into a corner. There was one thing new—sex.

Sex is a baffling thing when it doesn't happen. I used to wake up in the morning, when I was married, and wonder if the whole world was crazy, whooping about sex all the time. It was like hearing all the time that stove polish was the greatest invention on earth.

Then it dawned on me that people—other women—were different than me. They could feel things I couldn't. And when I started reading books I ran into the words "frigid," "rejected," and "lesbian." I wondered if I was all three of those things.

A man who had kissed me once had said it was very possible I was a lesbian because I apparently had no response to males—meaning him. I didn't contradict him because I didn't know what I was. There were times even when I didn't feel human and times when all I could think of was dying. There was also the sinister fact that a well-made woman had always thrilled me to look at.

Now, having fallen in love, I knew what I was. It wasn't a lesbian. The world and its excitement over sex didn't seem crazy. In fact, it didn't seem crazy enough.

There was only one cloud in my paradise, and it kept

growing. At first nothing had mattered to me except my own love. After a few months I began to look at *his* love. I looked, listened, and looked, and I couldn't tell myself more than he told me. I couldn't tell if he really loved me.

He grinned a lot when we were together and kidded me a lot. I knew he liked me and was happy to be with me. But his love didn't seem anything like mine. Most of his talk to me was a form of criticism. He criticized my mind. He kept pointing out how little I knew and how unaware of life I was. It was sort of true. I tried to know more by reading books. I had a new friend, Natasha Lytess. She was an acting coach and a woman of deep culture. She told me what to read. I read Tolstoy and Turgenev. They excited me, and I couldn't lay a book down till I'd finished it. And I would go around dreaming of all the characters I'd read and hearing them talk to each other. But I didn't feel that my mind was improving.

I never complained about his criticism, but it hurt me. His cynicism hurt me, too.

I'd say, "I've never felt like this before."

And he'd answer, "You will, again."

"I don't know," I'd say. "I just know that this is everything."

He'd answer, "You mustn't take a few sensations so seriously." Then he'd ask, "What's most important in life to you?"

"You are," I'd say.

"After I'm gone," he'd smile.

I'd cry.

"You cry too easily," he'd say. "That's because your mind isn't developed. Compared to your breasts it's embryonic." I couldn't contradict him because I had to look up that word in a dictionary. "Your mind is inert," he'd say. "You never think about life. You just float through it on that pair of water wings you wear."

Alone, I would lie awake repeating all he'd said. I'd think, "He can't love me or he wouldn't be so conscious of my faults. How can he love me if I'm such a goof to him?"

I didn't mind being a goof if only he loved me. I felt when we were together that I walked in the gutter and he on the sidewalk. All I did was keep looking up to see if there was love in his eyes.

We were in my room one night, and he started talking about our future.

"I've thought of us getting married," he said, "but I'm afraid it's impossible."

I didn't say anything.

"It would be all right for me," he said, "but I keep thinking of my son. If we were married and anything should happen to me—such as my dropping dead—it would be very bad for him."

"Why?" I asked.

"It wouldn't be right for him to be brought up by a woman like you," he said. "It would be unfair to him."

After he left, I cried all night, not over what he had said but over what I had to do. I had to leave him.

The moment I thought it, I realized I'd known it for a long time. That's why I'd been sad—and desperate. That's why I had tried to make myself more and more beautiful for him, why I had clung to him as if I were half mad. Because I had known it was ending.

He didn't love me. A man can't love a woman for whom he feels half contempt. He can't love her if his mind is ashamed of her.

When I saw him again the next day I said good-bye to him. He stood staring at me while I told him how I felt. I cried, sobbed, and ended up in his arms.

But a week later I said good-bye again. This time I walked out of his house with my head up. Two days later I was back. There were a third and fourth good-bye. But it was like rushing to the edge of a roof to jump off. I stopped each time and didn't jump, and turned to him and begged him to hold me. It's hard to do something that hurts your heart, especially when it's a new heart and you think that one hurt may kill it.

Finally I left him, and two days passed and I was still away. I sat in my room watching myself.

"Stick it out another day," I'd say. "The hurt's getting less already."

It wasn't, but I stuck it out a third and fourth day. Then he came after me. He knocked on my door. I walked to the door and leaned against it.

"It's me," he said.

"I know."

"Please let me in," he said.

I didn't answer. He started banging on the door. When I heard him banging, I knew I was through with my love affair. I knew I was over it. The pain was still there but it would go away.

"Please," he kept saying, "I want to talk to you."

"I don't want to see you," I said. "Please go away."

He raised his voice and banged harder.

"But you're mine," he cried at me. "You can't leave me out here."

The neighbors opened their doors. One of them yelled she'd call the police if he didn't quit making a disturbance.

He went away.

He came back again—as I had done before. He loved me now. He met me in the street and walked beside me pouring his heart out. But it didn't mean anything. When his hand gripped my arm, my arm didn't buzz, my heart didn't leap.

D URING THE time I loved this man, I kept looking for work. I had forgotten about my "career." I looked for work because I thought he would love me more if I were employed. I felt it made him a little nervous to have me just sitting around and doing nothing but wait for him. A man sometimes gets guilty and angry if you love him too much.

Besides I was broke. I was living on money I could borrow.

Someone I met at a lunch counter told me they were making retakes on a movie called *Love Happy* and needed a girl for a bit part. Harpo and Groucho Marx were in the movie.

I went on the set and found the producer Lester Cowan in charge. He was a small man with dark, sad eyes. He introduced me to Groucho and Harpo Marx. It was like meeting familiar characters out of Mother Goose. There they were with the same happy, crazy look I had seen on the screen. They both smiled at me as if I were a piece of French pastry.

"This is the young lady for the office bit," said Mr. Cowan.

Groucho stared thoughtfully at me.

"Can you walk?" he demanded.

I nodded.

"I am not referring to the type of walking my Tante Zippa has mastered," said Groucho. "This role calls for a young lady who can walk by me in such a manner as to arouse my elderly libido and cause smoke to issue from my ears."

Harpo honked a horn at the end of his cane and grinned at me.

I walked the way Groucho wanted.

"Exceedingly well done," he beamed.

Harpo's horn honked three times, and he stuck his fingers in his mouth and blew a piercing whistle.

"Walk again," said Mr. Cowan.

I walked up and down in front of the three men. They stood grinning.

"It's Mae West, Theda Bara, and Bo Peep all rolled into one," said Groucho. "We shoot the scene tomorrow morning. Come early."

"And don't do any walking in any unpoliced areas," said Harpo.

I played the next day; Groucho directed me. It was hardly more than a walk-on, but Mr. Cowan, the producer, said I had the makings of a star and that he was going to do something about it right away.

When you're broke and a nobody and a man tells you that, he becomes a genius in your eyes. But nothing happened for a week. I sat every evening listening to my lover argue about my various shortcomings, and I remained blissfully happy.

Then one morning I found my name in the headline of Louella Parsons' movie column in the *Los Angeles Examiner*. I was so excited I fell out of bed. The headline said Lester Cowan had put me under contract to star in a forthcoming movie.

That was something to read! I dressed and made up quicker than a fireman and squandered my last two dollars on a taxi.

Mr. Cowan was in his office.

"What can I do for you, Miss Monroe?" he inquired. He always spoke like a gentleman.

"I would like to sign the contract," I said, "that I read about in Miss Louella Parsons' column."

"I haven't drawn it up yet," Mr. Cowan smiled. "It will take a while."

"How much are you going to pay me?" I asked. Mr. Cowan said he hadn't decided on a figure yet.

"A hundred dollars a week will be enough," I said.

"We'll see about it," Mr. Cowan replied. "You just go home and wait till you hear from me. I'll send for you."

"Your word of honor?" I asked.

"Word of honor," Mr. Cowan said solemnly.

I borrowed two dollars from a friend I knew sort of and hurried off to a jewelry store. I had never given my lover a present of any kind, due to my financial condition. Now I saw a chance to get him something beautiful.

I showed the man in the jewelry store the headline in Louella Parsons' column and my picture in it.

"I'm Marilyn Monroe," I said. "You can compare me to the photograph."

"I can see you are," the jeweler agreed.

"I haven't any money now," I said. "In fact I have less than two dollars in the world. But you can see from what it says in Miss Parsons' column that I am on my way to stardom and will soon receive a great deal of money from Mr. Cowan."

The jeweler nodded.

"Of course, I haven't signed the contract yet, or even seen it." I didn't want him to misunderstand anything. "And Mr. Cowan, whom I just saw, said it would take a while—but I thought perhaps you might trust me. I want to buy a present for someone very dear to me."

The man smiled and said he would trust me and that I could pick out anything in the store.

I picked out an object that cost five hundred dollars and ran to my lover's home and waited for him.

He was quite overcome by the beauty of my present. Nobody had ever given him such an expensive object before.

"But you haven't engraved it," he said. "From Marilyn to _____ with love. Or something like that."

My heart almost stopped as he said this.

"I was going to have it engraved," I answered, "but changed my mind."

"Why?" he asked. He looked very tenderly at me.

"Because you'll leave me someday," I said, "and you'll have some other girl to love. And thus you wouldn't be able to use my present if my name was on it. This way you can always use it, as if it were something you'd bought yourself."

Usually when a woman says that sort of thing to her lover she expects to be contradicted and soothed out of her fears. I didn't. At night I lay in bed and cried. To love without hope is a sad thing for the heart.

It took me two years to pay the jeweler the five hundred dollars. By the time I had paid the last twenty-five dollar installment, my lover was married to another woman.

M R. COWAN kept his word and sent for me. He wasn't ready to use me as a star, seeing he had no picture to put me in. But he would like to engage me to exploit the movie *Love Happy*.

"But I don't know how to exploit a picture," I said.

"You don't have to know," Mr. Cowan replied. "All you have to do is to be Marilyn Monroe."

He explained that I would travel from city to city, put up in the finest hotels, meet the press, give out interviews, and pose for photographers.

"You will have a chance to see the world," Mr. Cowan said, "and it will broaden your horizons."

I agreed to exploit the picture, and Mr. Cowan agreed to pay all my traveling expenses and give me a salary of a hundred dollars a week.

One of the reasons I accepted the job was that I thought it would make my lover realize how much he loved me—if I went away for a few weeks. He didn't seem to be able to realize it with me hanging around twenty-four hours a day. I had read that men love you more if they can be made a little uncertain about owning you. But reading something is one thing, doing it is quite another. Besides, I could never pretend to feel something I didn't feel. I could never make love if I didn't love, and if I loved I could no more hide the fact than change the color of my eyes.

The day before I left for New York to start the *Love Happy* exploitation tours of the U.S.A. I suddenly realized that I had almost no wardrobe. I called on Mr. Cowan and told him about this.

"I won't be much of an advertisement in one old suit," I said.

Mr. Cowan smiled and agreed I had better have a larger wardrobe. He gave me seventy-five dollars to outfit myself for the tour. I rushed over to the May Company store and bought three woolen suits for twenty-five dollars apiece.

I bought the woolen suits because I remembered that New York and Chicago were in the North. I had seen them in the movies blanketed with snow. In my excitement over going to see these great cities for the first time I forgot it was summertime there as well as in Los Angeles.

On the way to New York I made plans of all the things I would see.

My lover had always said, one of the reasons you have nothing to talk about is you've never been anywhere or seen anything.

I was going to remedy that.

When the train stopped in New York I could hardly breathe, it was so hot. It was hotter than I had ever known it to be in Hollywood. The woolen suit made me feel as if I was wearing an oven.

Mr. Cowan's press agent, who was supervising my exploitation trip, rose to the situation.

"We must make capital out of what we have," he explained. So he arranged for me to pose on the train steps with perspiration running down my face and an ice cream cone in each hand.

The caption for the pictures read: "Marilyn Monroe, the hottest thing in pictures, cooling off."

That "cooling off" idea became sort of the basis for my exploitation work.

A half hour after arriving in New York I was led into an elegant suite in the Sherry-Netherland Hotel and told to put on a bathing suit.

More photographers arrived and took more pictures of me "cooling off."

I spent several days in New York looking at the walls of my elegant suite and the little figures of people fifteen stories below. All sorts of people came to interview me, not only newspapers and magazine reporters but exhibitors and other exploitation people from United Artists.

I asked questions about the Statue of Liberty and what were the best shows to see and the most glamorous cafés to go to. But I saw nothing and went nowhere.

Finally I got so tired of sitting around perspiring in one of my three woolen suits, that I complained.

"It seems to me," I said to the United Artists' representatives who were having dinner with me in my suite, "that I ought to have something more attractive to wear in the evening."

They agreed and bought me a cotton dress at a wholesale shop. It had a low-cut neck and blue polka dots. They explained, also, that cotton was much more chic in the big cities than silk. I did like the red velvet belt that came with it.

The next stop was Detroit, and then Cleveland, Chicago, Milwaukee, and Rockford. It was the same story in each of them. I was taken to a hotel, rushed into a bathing suit, given a fan and photographers arrived. The hottest thing in pictures was cooling off again.

In Rockford I decided that I had seen enough of the world. Also, due to my moving around continually and to the confusion this seemed to arouse in Mr. Cowan's bookkeeping department, I had not received any salary whatsoever. The salary, it was explained to me, would be waiting for me at the next stop. As a result I didn't have fifty cents to spend on myself during my grand tour.

After sitting in the lobby of a Rockford movie theater, "keeping cool" in a bathing suit and handing out orchids to "my favorite male moviegoers" I told the press agent that I would like to return to Hollywood.

The tour, in a way, was a failure. When I got back I didn't seem to have any more to talk about than before. And absence didn't seem to have made my friend's heart grow any fonder.

ONE DAY I was sitting in an office of the William Morris Agency. A very short man was behind a large desk. He was talking to me in a quiet voice and looking at me with kind eyes. He was John Hyde, one of the most important talent scouts in Hollywood. Everyone called him Johnny Hyde because of the friendly look he had for everyone.

"You're going to be a great movie star," Johnny Hyde said to me. "I know. Many years ago I discovered a girl like you and brought her to Metro—Lana Turner. You're better. You'll go farther. You've got more."

"Then why can't I get a job?" I asked. "Just to make enough money to eat on."

"It's hard for a star to get an eating job," said Johnny Hyde. "A star is only good as a star. You don't fit into anything less."

I laughed for the first time in months. Johnny Hyde didn't laugh with me. He kept looking at me, and looking.

"Yes," he said, "it's there. I can feel it. I see a hundred actresses a week. They haven't got what you have. Do you know what I'm talking about?"

"Yes," I said. "I used to feel it myself once. When I was a kid, when I first started. But I haven't felt it for some time now. I've been too busy having troubles."

"Love trouble?" he said.

I said, "Yes."

"Come around tomorrow, and we'll talk again," said Johnny Hyde.

I had made another friend, a woman who was the head of M.G.M. talent scout department. Her name was Lucille Ryman.

Miss Ryman had not only been kind to me and loaned me money and things to wear, but she had also assured me I was going to be a star.

One day Miss Ryman called me up.

"There's a part for you in John Huston's picture *The Asphalt Jungle* that's perfect for you," she said. "It's not a big part, but you'll be bound to make a big hit in it. Tell your agent to get in touch with Mr. Huston. I've already discussed you with him."

Johnny Hyde brought me to Mr. Huston's office. Arthur Hornblow, the producer of the picture, was also present.

Mr. Huston was an exciting looking man. He was tall, long-faced, and his hair was mussed. He interrupted everybody with outbursts of laughter as if he were drunk. But he wasn't drunk. He was just happy for some mysterious reason, and he was also a genius—the first I had ever met.

I had met Mr. Zanuck, of course, who was also widely regarded as a genius. But he was a different type of genius—the genius of being in a position to give orders to everybody in a studio. In Hollywood this type of genius is the most highly esteemed and makes the most money. But, in a way, it is not genius at all. It's more having the best job—and the best people working for you.

Mr. Huston gave me a copy of the script. Unlike Mr. Zanuck, he did not believe that actresses shouldn't be allowed to know what they were going to act in. I took it home and my friend Natasha Lytess agreed to coach me.

"Do you think you can do it?" Johnny Hyde asked me. "You have to break up in it and cry and sob."

"I thought you thought I was a star," I said to him, "and I could do anything."

"You can," he said, "but I can't help worrying."

At first I felt that Johnny had lost faith in me. Then I realized he was just being "too close" to me and that he was worrying with my nerves and fears.

I studied the part for several days and then returned to

Mr. Huston's office to read for him. Several other men were present, including Mr. Hornblow who was the only bald-headed man I had ever seen who looked more elegant than men with hair. In fact he seemed more like some cultured foreign diplomat than a mere movie producer.

They were all friendly and made jokes, but I couldn't smile. I felt, also, that I would never be able to recite a line. A pulse was pounding in my stomach. I couldn't have been more frightened if I were about to step in front of a locomotive to get run over.

"Well," said Mr. Huston, "do you like the part?"

I nodded. My mouth was too dry to try talking.

"Do you think you can do it?"

I nodded again.

I felt sick. I had told myself a million times that I was an actress. I had practiced acting for years. Here, finally, was my first chance at a real acting part with a great director to direct me. And all I could do is stand with quivering knees and a quivering stomach and nod my head like a wooden toy.

Luckily the men fell to making more jokes and seemed to forget about me. They laughed and kidded as if nothing important was involved. But I could feel that behind his burst of laughter Mr. Huston was watching me and waiting for me.

I felt desperate. What was the use of reading in a shaking voice like a terrified amateur? Mr. Huston caught my eye and grinned.

"We're waiting, Miss Monroe," he said.

"I don't think I'm going to be any good," I answered.

Everybody stopped talking and looked at me.

"Would you mind if I read the part lying on the floor?" I blurted out.

"Why, not at all," Mr. Huston replied gallantly. "Bill, here, will cue you."

I stretched myself out on the floor and Bill crouched down beside me. I felt much better. I had rehearsed the part lying on a couch, as the directions indicated. There wasn't any couch in the office. Lying on the floor was almost the same thing, however.

I went through the part, with the crouching Bill reading Louis Calhern's lines. When I finished I said, "Oh, let me do it again."

"If you want to," said Mr. Huston, "but there's no need."

I did it again.

When I stood up Mr. Huston said, "You were in after the first reading. Go fix yourself up with the wardrobe department."

I knew this part wouldn't be cut out of the picture because it was vital to the plot. I was the reason one of the stars, Louis Calhern, committed suicide. My characterization was Mae West, Theda Bara, and Bo Peep—in tight silk lounging pajamas.

UP—AND DOWN
AGAIN

I N A MOVIE you act in little bits and pieces. You say two lines, and they *"cut."* They relight, set up the camera in another place—and you act two more lines. You walk five feet, and they say "cut." The minute you get going good in your characterization, they cut.

But it doesn't matter. There's no audience watching you. There's nobody to act *for* except yourself. It's like the games you play when you're a child and pretend to be somebody else. Usually, it's even almost the same sort of story you used to make up as a child—about meeting somebody who fell in love with you because, despite everything they'd heard against you, you were a good girl with a heart of gold. I've wondered sometimes when I've been in a picture if the people making it hadn't had their children ghostwrite it for them, and I've thought, "Wouldn't it be wonderful if I accidentally opened a door and there they were—the children who really make up the movies—a room full of eight- and nine-year-old kids. Then I could go to the studio head and say, 'I'd like to play in something a little better than the script you've given me. Something a little more human and true to life.' And when he answered me that the script was made up by the finest brains in the country and I was a fool to criticize it, I'd tell him I knew his secret—the room full of babies who were creating all the movies. And he'd turn pale and give in, and I'd be given a script written by some adult and become a real actress."

I didn't have this daydream during *Asphalt Jungle* because it was an adult script. There was also an audience watching me act—an audience of one, the director. A director like Mr. Huston makes your work exciting. Some directors seem more interested in photographing the scenery than the actors. They keep moving the camera around saying, "Here's a wonderful shot." Or, "This is a superb set-up. We'll be able to get the fireplace and the Oriental mask in the frame." Or they say, "That'll cut beautifully. It'll give us a fast tempo."

You feel they're more interested in their directing than they are in your acting. They want the Front Office to praise *them* when the rushes are shown. Mr. Huston wasn't like that. He was interested in the acting I did. He not only watched it, he was part of it. And even though my part was a minor one, I felt as if I were the most important performer in the picture when I was before the camera. This was because everything I did was important to the director, just as important as everything the stars of the picture did.

Johnny Hyde was as excited as I was during the shooting. He kept telling me, "This is it, honey. You're in. Everybody is crazy about your work."

When the picture was previewed, all the studio heads went to see it. It was a fine picture. I was thrilled by it. The biggest thrill, though, was myself. The audience whistled at me. They made "wolf noises." They laughed happily when I spoke. They liked me very much.

It's a nice sensation to please an audience. I sat in the theater with Johnny Hyde. He held my hand. We didn't say anything on the way home. He sat in my room beaming at me. It was as if he had made good on the screen, not me. It was not only because I was his client and his "discovery." His heart was happy for me. I could feel his unselfishness and his deep kindness. No man had ever looked on me with such kindness. He not only knew me, he knew Norma Jean, too. He knew all the pain and all the desperate things in me. When he put his arms around me and said he loved me, I knew it was true. Nobody had ever loved me like that. I wished with all my heart that I could love him back.

I told him about my love affair that had just ended and about all the pain I had felt. The affair was over in every way but one. It made it hard to love again. Johnny was even kind about this. He didn't scream and carry on. He understood. He didn't blame or criticize. Life was full of mix-ups and wrong starts, he said. He would wait for my heart to get strong again and wait for me to love him, if I could.

Kindness is the strangest thing to find in a lover—or in anybody. Johnny's kindness made him seem the most wonderful human being I'd ever met.

"The first thing to do," he said to me the next day, "is get you a contract with Metro."

"Do you think you can?" I asked.

"They've got a new star on their hands," said Johnny, "and they know it. Everybody is raving about your work. Most of all, you saw and heard that audience. They bought you as I've never seen any small part player bought in a picture before."

A week later Johnny said to me, "I don't want you to feel depressed, honey. We've had a temporary setback."

"Metro doesn't want me," I said.

"You guessed it," Johnny smiled at me. "It's fantastic. I've been talking to Dore Schary all week. He likes your work. He thinks you've done a wonderful job, in fact. But he said you're not star material. He says you're not photogenic, that you haven't got the sort of looks that make a movie star."

"Maybe he's right," I said. "Mr. Zanuck said the same thing when 20th dropped me."

"He's wrong," said Johnny. "And so was Zanuck. I have to laugh when I think how wrong they are and how they'll both eat their words someday—and someday soon."

Johnny laughed, but I didn't. It was frightening—to be up so high in your hopes and then take another tumble back to no work, no prospects, no money, and nowhere. But I didn't quite take the full tumble this time. I wasn't alone. I had Johnny with me. I wasn't merely Johnny's client, or even his sweetie. I was a Cause he had. That's how my friend swarmed all over the studios.

My heart ached with gratitude, and I would have cut my head off for him. But the love he hoped for wasn't in me. You might as well try to make yourself fly as to make yourself love. But I felt everything else toward Johnny Hyde, and I was always happy to be with him. It was like being with a whole family and belonging to a full set of relatives.

IT'S HARD to hope with somebody else's heart and be happy with somebody else's daydreams. But Johnny made me happy and kept me believing in myself. I didn't run around the studios job-hunting anymore. Johnny did that. I stayed home and took dramatic lessons and read books.

One of them excited me more than any other I had read. It was *The Autobiography of Lincoln Steffens*. It was the first book I'd read that seemed to tell the truth about people and life. It was bitter but strong. It didn't just echo the half lies I'd always heard—about how people loved each other and how justice always triumphed and how the important people of the nation always did the right thing for their country.

Lincoln Steffens knew all about poor people and about injustice. He knew about the lies people used to get ahead, and how smug rich people sometimes were. It was almost as if he'd lived the hard way I'd lived. I loved his book. Reading it I forgot all about not having a job and not being "photogenic."

But Johnny didn't forget.

"We've landed a good one," he reported one evening. "I didn't want to talk about it till I was sure. I'm sure now. It's the new Joseph Mankiewicz picture called *All About Eve*. It's not a big part but it will establish you at 20th."

"But they don't like me there," I said.

"They will," said Johnny.

Mr. Mankiewicz was a different sort of director than Mr. Huston. He wasn't as exciting, and he was more talkative. But he was intelligent and sensitive. I felt happy on the set, and, with Johnny Hyde's help, I was able to daydream again.

The studio was always cooking up little publicity stories for the different people under its roof. I was eager for publicity, but there was one kind I refused to accept. This was the publicity you got as a result of being seen in a café at night with a fellow actor. The columnists would then hint that you and the young actor were setting out on a romance.

I didn't like going to fancy cafés and sitting around with some ambitious profile. I didn't like people thinking of me as being romantic about somebody I didn't know. And I knew Johnny wouldn't like it. So I stayed out of the cafés and the movie columns as a romance dizzy starlet.

The only trouble I had during the making of *Eve* came from Zsa Zsa Gabor (again) and Lincoln Steffens. They were both mild troubles but they confused me. The Lincoln Steffens trouble began when Mr. Mankiewicz asked me one day what was the book I was reading on the set. I told him it was the Steffens autobiography and I started raving about it. Mr. Mankiewicz took me aside and gave me a quiet lecture.

"I wouldn't go around raving about Lincoln Steffens," he said. "It's certain to get you into trouble. People will begin to talk of you as a radical."

"A radical what?" I asked.

"A political radical," Mr. Mankiewicz said. "Don't tell me you haven't heard of Communists."

"Not much," I said.

"Don't you read the papers?"

"I skip the parts I don't like," I said.

"Well, lay off boosting Mr. Steffens, or you'll get into bad trouble," said Mr. Mankiewicz.

I thought this was a very personal attitude on Mr. Mankiewicz's part and, that genius though he was, of a sort, he was badly frightened by the Front Office or something. I couldn't imagine anybody picking on me because I admired Lincoln Steffens. The only other political figure I'd ever admired was Abraham Lincoln. I used to read everything I could find about him. He was the only famous American who seemed most like me, at least in his childhood.

A few days later the publicity department asked me to write out a list of the ten greatest men in the world. I wrote the name Lincoln Steffens down first and the publicity man shook his head.

"We'll have to omit that one," he said. "We don't want anybody investigating our Marilyn."

I saw then that it wasn't just a personal thing with Mr. Mankiewicz but that maybe everybody in Hollywood was just as scared of being associated with Lincoln Steffens. So I didn't say anything more about him, to anybody, not even to Johnny. I didn't want to get *him* in trouble. But I continued to read the second volume secretly and kept both volumes hidden under my bed. Hiding Lincoln Steffens under my bed was the first underhanded thing I'd ever done—since my meeting with little George in the tall grass.

The third and last act, I hope, of my one-sided Gabor feud took place during *Eve*. I was sitting in the studio commissary having lunch with Mr. George Sanders, who was the hero of the picture. We had sat down at the same table more or less by accident, having entered the commissary together, also by accident. The whole thing was an accident. Mr. Sanders was just beginning to eat his chicken salad when the cashier's assistant came to the table and told him he was wanted on the telephone.

About five minutes later Mr. Sanders returned to our table, called for the waitress, and paid his check.

"If you'll pardon me, I must go now," he said to me.

"But you haven't had your lunch yet," I said.

"I'm not hungry," said Mr. Sanders.

"You said you were terribly hungry when you sat down," I said, "and would have to be careful not to overeat. Why don't you just have a bite so you'll have some strength for your big scene this afternoon."

Mr. Sanders looked so pale that I was really worried.

"Unless you're sick," I said.

"I'm in perfect health," said Mr. Sanders, "and I must leave now."

"I'll drive you over to the stage," I said. "I came in my car, and I noticed you walked."

"Oh no, thank you very much," said Mr. Sanders. "I don't want to bother you."

"It's no bother at all," I said. "I've finished my lunch. It's a shame for you to walk all that distance on an empty stomach."

I stood up and started to leave the commissary with Mr. Sanders, but he pulled briskly away from me and I couldn't have kept up with him unless I broke into a trot. So I walked out slowly alone wondering what I had done to make Mr. Sanders rush away from my company.

On the set ten minutes later, Mr. Sanders' stand-in, who was almost as charming and polite as the star himself, came to me and said, "Mr. Sanders has asked me to request of you that hereafter when you say good morning or good-bye to him, you will make those salutations from afar."

I turned red at being insulted like this but I suddenly realized what had happened. Mr. Sanders' wife, Zsa Zsa Gabor, obviously had a spy on the set, and this spy had flashed the news to her that he was sitting at a table with me, and Miss Gabor had telephoned him immediately and given him a full list of instructions. I laughed when I realized this, and I thought about it for some time. I could imagine loving a man with my whole heart and soul and wanting to be with him every minute. But I couldn't imagine being so jealous of him that I would have spies planted everywhere to watch him. But maybe I was too young to understand about such things.

22

I COULD never be attracted to a man who had perfect teeth. A man with perfect teeth always alienated me. I don't know what it is but it has something to do with the kind of men I have known who had perfect teeth. They weren't so perfect elsewhere.

There's another sort of man I've never liked—the sort that's afraid of insulting you. They always end up by insulting you worse than anybody. I much prefer a man to be a wolf and, if he has decided to make a pass at me, to make it and have it over with.

First of all, a pass is never entirely unpleasant because men who make passes are usually bright and good-looking. Secondly, you don't have to sit around with a wolf and listen to a lot of double-talk about income taxes and what's wrong with the situation in India while he gets up enough courage to get into action.

Worse, though, than these double-talkers are the Good Samaritan pass-makers. These are the ones who are interested in my career and want to do something big for me. They are usually married men, of course. I don't mean that married men are all hypocrites. Many of them are straightforward wolves. They will ask you straightforwardly to overlook the fact that they are wedded to wives who seem to adore them—and go on from there.

There is variety among men, always. Even the wolves differ from each other a little bit. Some wolves like to talk about sex a great deal. Others are terribly polite about saying anything offensive, and act as if they were inviting you to some important social event.

The nicest thing about wolves is that they seldom get

angry or critical of you. This doesn't apply, of course, if you succumb to them. Then they are likely to lose their tempers, but for a different reason than most men. A wolf is inclined to get very angry if a woman makes the mistake of falling in love with him. But it would take a rather foolish woman to do that.

The only time I ever knew a wolf really to lose his temper was the time a girl friend of mine dated a famous director.

"Here's the key to my apartment," she told him. "I have a dinner date. You go there and wait for me. I'll join you around ten-thirty."

The famous director went to her apartment. He undressed and lay down in bed. He had brought a script along to read. At eleven-thirty he had finished reading the script. The phone rang. A man's voice inquired for Miss B.

"She is not home yet," the famous director said.

After that the phone kept ringing every fifteen minutes. There was a way to shut off the ringing, but the director didn't know where the switch was, so he had to keep answering. Each time it was another wolf like himself asking for Miss B.

I don't know exactly what happened, but when Miss B. came home around 4 A.M. she found the bed empty and the telephone had been torn from the wall. The note he left behind read, "Enclosed is the key to your apartment. What you need is not a lover but an answering service."

But to return to the Good Samaritan pass-makers, they are not only the worst but the most numerous. When they get old enough they graduate into talking to you like a father. When a man says to me, "I'm giving you exactly the same advice I'd give my own daughter," I know he isn't "dangerous" anymore—that is, if he actually has a daughter.

The chief drawback with men is that they are too talkative. I don't mean intellectual men who are full of ideas and information about life. It's always a delight to hear such men talk because they are not talking boastfully. The overtalkative men who bore me are the ones who talk about themselves. Sometimes they confine themselves to plain, uninterrupted boasting. They'll sit for an hour telling you how smart they are and how stupid everybody else around them is. Sometimes they don't even boast but give you an inside on what they like to eat and where they've been in the last five years.

Such men are a total loss. A man can please a woman by talking about himself after they're lovers. Then he can confess all his sins and tell her of all the other women he has had.

Lovers who don't do that and who keep silent on the subject of their pasts are very rare. And they are not too bright, either. Sometimes men like to hear about a woman's past love affairs, but it's better for a woman not to take a chance and tell. Unless she is truly in love and wishes to belong to the man entirely—and doesn't mind a long spell of hollering.

Men who think that a woman's past love affairs lessen her love for them are usually stupid and weak. A woman can bring a new love to each man she loves, providing there are not too many.

The most unsatisfactory men are those who pride themselves on their virility and regard sex as if it were some form of athletics at which you win cups. It is a woman's spirit and mood a man has to stimulate in order to make sex interesting. The real lover is the man who can thrill you by just touching your head or smiling into your eyes—or by just staring into space.

I HAVE always had a talent for irritating women since I was fourteen. Wives have a tendency to go off like burglar alarms when they see their husbands talking to me. Even young and pretty Hollywood "maidens" greet me with more sneer than smile.

This sort of sex fear that women often feel when I walk into their barnyard has different effects on me. I find it flattering—and upsetting. I find it also mysterious. Women don't resent me because I'm prettier or better shaped than they are—or show more of myself to the male eye. I've seen women at parties who had only enough clothes on to keep from being arrested, and I've heard such party-nudists buzzing about how vulgar I was. They were showing more leg, more bosom, and more spinal column than I was—and I was the "vulgar" one!

Women also don't like the way I talk—even when I'm not talking to their husbands or lovers. One angry woman said my voice was "too premeditated." I found out she meant I was putting on a sort of bedroom drawl. This isn't true. The chief difference between my voice and the voices of most women I've seen is that I use mine less. I can't chatter if I wanted to. I can't pretend to laugh and be full of some sort of foolish good spirits when I'm in company. Standing around at a party looking serious attracts unfavorable feminine comment. They think I'm plotting something, and usually the same thing—how to steal their gentlemen friends from under their noses.

I don't mind their thinking that. I would rather a thousand women were jealous of me than I was jealous of one of them. I've been jealous, and it's no fun.

Sometimes I've been to a party where no one spoke to me a whole evening. The men, frightened by their wives or sweeties, would give me a wide berth. And the ladies would gang up in a corner to discuss my dangerous character.

Being given the social cold shoulder like that never made me too unhappy. I've done most of my thinking at such parties, standing in a corner with a cocktail glass in hand and nobody to talk to. I've thought about women. Their jealousy had little to do with me. It comes out of their realizing their own shortcomings. Men have told me a lot about women—how lame their love-making often is, how they mistake hysteria for passion and nagging for devotion. Looking at me, women think I'm different than they are in such matters, and this makes them angry.

When I see women frowning in my direction and cutting me up among themselves, I really feel sorry—not for them but for their menfolk. I have a feeling that such women are poor lovers and sexual cripples. The only thing they are able to give a man is a guilt complex. If they are able to make him feel that he is a bad husband or an unappreciative lover, then they consider themselves "successful."

J OHNNY HYDE's kindness changed the outside world for me, but it didn't touch my inner world. I tried hard to love him. He was not only kind, but loyal and wise and devoted.

He took me everywhere. People admired him and accepted me as his fiancée. But I wasn't that. Johnny asked me to marry him. It wouldn't be a long marriage, he said, because he had a heart condition. I never could say yes.

"Tell me again why you won't marry me," he would smile at me.

"Because it wouldn't be fair," I'd answer him. "I don't love you, Johnny. That means if I married you I might meet some other man and fall in love with him. I don't want that ever to happen. If I marry a man I want to feel I'll always be faithful to him—and never love anyone else."

Johnny was hurt by what I said, but his love wasn't because he knew I was honest. He knew he could trust me. He was never jealous because of anything I had done. It was always because of what I might do. Most men have been jealous for the same reason. I've liked their jealousy. Often it was the only sincere thing about their love. Most men judge your importance in their lives by how much you can hurt them, not by how happy you can make them. But there was one kind of jealousy I never liked. It was the jealousy that kept a man asking questions about other men, and never letting up, and wanting to know more and more details. I felt then that my jealous friend was more interested in those men than in me, and that he was hiding a homosexuality in his pretended jealousy pains.

I did all I could to lessen Johnny Hyde's fears. I never

went out with other men. I was as faithful to him as he was kind to me.

Johnny Hyde gave me more than his kindness and love. He was the first man I had ever known who understood me. Most men (and women) thought I was scheming and two-faced. No matter how truthfully I spoke to them or how honestly I behaved, they always believed I was trying to fool them.

When I talk I have a habit of not finishing sentences, and this gives the impression I'm telling lies. I'm not. I'm just not finishing sentences. Johnny knew that I didn't tell lies and that I wasn't planning to fool him.

The truth is I've never fooled anyone. I've let men sometimes fool themselves. Men sometimes didn't bother to find out who and what I was. Instead they would invent a character for me. I wouldn't argue with them. They were obviously loving somebody I wasn't. When they found this out, they would blame me for disillusioning them—and fooling them.

I have even tried to be straightforward with women. This is more difficult than being straightforward with men. Men are often pleased when you tell them the truth about how you feel. But very few women want to hear any truth —if it's going to be in any way annoying. As far as I can make out, women's friendships with each other are based on a gush of lies and pretty speeches that mean nothing. You'd think they were all wolves trying to seduce each other the way they flatter and flirt when they're together.

I found a few exceptions. There was one woman who helped me a great deal in my early Hollywood days—when I used to dream of getting enough money to own more than one brassiere. She gave me money and let me live in her home and wear her gowns and furs. She did this because she sincerely liked me and because she believed I had talent and would become a star some day. I'll call her Della and so be able to write about her without embarrassing her.

Della was married to an important movie actor. He was not only a star but a man. This is unusual, not because men movie actors are inclined to be pansies, but because acting is a feminine art. When a man has to paint his face and pose and strut and pretend emotions, and exhibit himself for applause, he certainly isn't doing what is normally masculine. He's "acting" just as women do in life. And he acquires a sort of womanish nature. He competes with women, even when he loves one of them.

Della's husband brought me to his home one day. I had caddied for him in a charity golf tournament.

"Here's a hungry little kitten," he said to his wife. "Take care of her. She's going places but she needs a little help."

THE PERSON I wanted to help most in my life—Johnny Hyde—remained someone for whom I could do almost nothing. He needed something I didn't have—love. And love is something you can't invent, no matter how much you want to.

He would say to me, "What kind of a man do you think you will fall in love with someday?" And I'd answer I didn't know. I would beg him not to think of any tomorrow but enjoy the life we were sharing together.

One evening in his home he started up the stairs to get me a book. I saw him stop on the landing and lean against the balustrade. I had seen my Aunt Ann do that a few months before she died of her heart attack.

I ran up to Johnny and put my arms around him and said, "Oh, Johnny, I'm sorry. I'm sorry you feel bad."

"I'll be all right," he said.

A week later Johnny Hyde began asking me again to marry him. He had been to a doctor, and the doctor had told him he didn't have long to live.

"I'm rich," he said to me. "I have almost a million dollars. If you marry me you'll inherit it when I die."

I had dreamed of money and longed for it. But the million dollars that Johnny Hyde now offered me meant nothing.

"I'll not leave you," I told him. "I'll never betray you. But I can't marry you, Johnny. Because you're going to get well. And sometime later I might fall in love."

He smiled at me.

"I won't get well," he said. "And I want you to have my money when I'm gone."

But I couldn't say yes. He was right. He didn't get well. A month later he went to the hospital. In the hospital he kept begging me to marry him, not for his sake anymore, but for mine. He wanted to think of me as never having any more hunger or poverty in my life.

But I still couldn't marry him. Joe Schenck argued with me to do it.

"What have you got to lose?" he asked.

"Myself," I said. "I'm only going to marry for one reason—love."

He asked me, "Which would you rather marry—a poor boy you loved or a rich man you liked?"

"A poor boy I loved," I said.

"I'm disappointed in you," Mr. Schenck said. "I thought you were a smart girl." But Mr. Schenck seemed to like me more after our talk.

Johnny Hyde died. His family wouldn't let me sit among them at the funeral. I sat in the back of the church among Johnny's acquaintances. When I passed by his coffin I felt such a sadness for Johnny Hyde that I forgot myself. I threw myself on the coffin and sobbed. I wished I was dead with him.

My great friend was buried. I was without his importance to fight for me and without his love to guide me. I cried for nights at a time. I never regretted the million dollars I had turned down. But I never stopped regretting Johnny Hyde—the kindest man in the world.

O NE EVENING I was listening to two friends of mine having an argument. We were having dinner in a small Italian restaurant. One of my friends was a writer. The other was a director.

The argument was whether Botticelli was a finer painter than Leonardo da Vinci. I kept my eyes wide with interest although I couldn't understand anything they were saying. To begin with I didn't know who Botticelli or da Vinci were.

"We're boring Marilyn," said the director. "I can always tell when she's bored to tears. She opens her eyes wide and parts her lips slightly with bogus eagerness."

"Let's talk about something closer to her than the Renaissance," said the writer. "How about sex?"

"At least I'll know what side you're on," I said.

But I didn't. The discussion about sex sounded completely unfamiliar. It had to do with Freud and Jung and a few other characters who seemed to me pretty mixed up.

Something occurred to me, however, as I sat listening to my two gay friends. I realized that about two-thirds of the time I hadn't the faintest idea of what people (even women) were talking about. There was no hiding from it—I was terribly dumb. I didn't know anything about painting, music, books, history, geography. I didn't even know anything about sports or politics.

When I arrived home I sat in my bed and asked myself if there was anything I did know. I couldn't think of anything—except acting. I knew about acting. It was a way to live in dreams for a few minutes at a time.

I decided to go to school. The next day I enrolled in the

University of Southern California. I subscribed for an art course.

I went to school every afternoon and often in the evening. The teacher was a woman. I was depressed by this at first because I didn't think a woman could teach me anything. But in a few days I knew differently.

She was one of the most exciting human beings I had ever met. She talked about the Renaissance and made it sound ten times more important than the Studio's biggest epic. I drank in everything she said. I met Michelangelo and Raphael and Tintoretto. There was a new genius to hear about every day.

At night I lay in bed wishing I could have lived in the Renaissance. Of course I would be dead now. But it seemed almost worth it.

After a few weeks I branched out as a student. I started buying books by Freud and some of his modern disciples. I read them till I got dizzy.

But I didn't have enough time. There were acting lessons and singing lessons, publicity interviews, sessions with photographers—and rehearsal of a movie.

I finally decided to postpone my intelligence, but I made a promise to myself I won't forget. I promised that in a few years after things had settled down I would start learning —everything. I would read all the books and find out about all the wonders there were in the world.

And when I sat among people I would not only understand what they were talking about. I'd be able to contribute a few words.

MY
JOAN CRAWFORD
"FEUD"

I MET Joan Crawford at Joe Schenck's house. She was an impressive woman. I admired her during dinner. I hoped that when I was her age I would keep my looks as well as she had.

Some movie stars don't seem like stars when you meet them, and some seem more like stars off the screen than on. I don't know which is better, but Miss Crawford was definitely the latter type. She was as much the movie star at Mr. Schenck's dinner table as she could have been electrifying a courtroom in a movie drama—even a little more.

I was pleased to see I had made an impression on Miss Crawford. She said to me after dinner, "I think I could help you a great deal if you would let me. For instance that white knitted dress you're wearing is utterly incorrect for a dinner of this kind."

It was the only good dress I owned. I wore it evenings as well as daytimes when I was going any place important, and I cleaned it myself everyday.

I looked at Miss Crawford's beautiful evening gown and understood what she meant.

"Taste," Miss Crawford went on, "is every bit as important as looks and figure." She smiled very kindly at me and asked, "Will you let me help you, my dear?"

I said I was flattered to have her offer to. We made a date to meet Sunday morning in church. It turned out that Miss Crawford and I went to the same church.

After the church service Miss Crawford said as we met coming out, "I'm so glad to see you. But you mustn't come to church in flat heels and a gray suit with black trimming.

If you wear gray you must wear different gray tones, but never black."

It was my only suit, but there was no sense defending it on that ground.

"Would you like to come to my house with me?" Miss Crawford asked.

I said I'd like to very much, and it was arranged that I should follow her car in mine.

I was excited at what I thought was going to happen. Miss Crawford, I felt pretty sure, was going to offer me some of her old ball gowns and ensembles that she'd grown tired of.

The house was very beautiful and elegant. We had lunch in the kitchen with Miss Crawford's four children and a beautiful white poodle.

After lunch Miss Crawford asked me to come upstairs to her room.

"Brown would look very good on you," she said. "I must show you the things I've been knitting."

She showed me a number of knitted dickies in different shades of brown and explained that they were to be worn under different shades of brown suits.

"The main thing about dressing well," Miss Crawford explained, "is to see that everything you wear is just right—that your shoes, stockings, gloves and bag all fit the suit you're wearing. Now what I would like you to do is to make a list of all the clothes in your wardrobe, and I'll make a list of all the things you need to buy and see that you buy the right things."

I didn't say anything. I usually didn't mind telling people I was broke and even trying to borrow a few dollars from them to tide me over. But for some reason I couldn't tell Miss Crawford that she had seen my wardrobe in full—the incorrect white knitted dress and the wrong gray suit.

"It's so easy not to look vulgar," Miss Crawford assured me, when I was ready to leave. "Do make out a list of all your things and let me guide you a bit. You'll be surprised at the results. And so will everyone else."

I don't know why I called Miss Crawford up again, except that I had promised I would. Maybe I was still hoping she would present me with some of her discarded ball gowns. I think, also, I had some intention of telling her the truth about not being able to buy any fancy clothes.

But when I heard Miss Crawford's voice on the phone, I had to start palavering as I'd done before. Had I made out that list of my wardrobe? No, I hadn't. That was very lazy of me. Yes, I knew. And I would make the list out in a few days and call her up again.

"Good," said Miss Crawford. "I'll be expecting to hear from you."

I didn't call Miss Crawford again. In fact, the next time I heard from Miss Crawford was in the newspapers. This was a year later. I'd gone to work at 20th Century-Fox again, and the Marilyn Monroe boom had started. I was all over the magazines and movie columns, and the fan mail at the studio was arriving in trucks.

Among the honors that were now showering on me was the privilege of presenting one of the Oscars to one of the Award winners at the Academy's annual affair.

I was frozen with fear the night of the Academy Award Ceremonies. I waited tremblingly for my turn to walk up to the platform and hand over the Oscar in my keeping. I prayed I wouldn't trip and fall and that my voice wouldn't disappear when I had to say my two lines.

When my turn came I managed to reach the platform, say my piece, and return to my table without any mishap.

Or so I thought until I read Joan Crawford's remarks in the morning papers.

I haven't saved the clippings, but I have sort of remembered what she said. She said that Marilyn Monroe's vulgar performance at the Academy affair was a disgrace to all of Hollywood. The vulgarity, she said, consisted of my wearing a dress too tight for me and wriggling my rear when I walked up holding one of the holy Oscars in my hand.

I was so surprised I could hardly believe what I was reading. I called up some friends who had seen me at the ceremony and asked them if it were true. They laughed. It wasn't true, they said. They advised me to forgive a lady who had once been young and seductive herself.

I have written out this accurate account of one of my "feuds" because it is typical. The feuds are all started by someone whom I have mysteriously offended—always a woman.

The truth is my tight dress and my wiggling were all in Miss Crawford's mind. She obviously had been reading too much about me.

Or maybe she was just annoyed because I had never brought her a list of my wardrobe.

UCCESS CAME to me in a rush. It surprised my
employers much more than it did me. Even when I had
played only bit parts in a few films, all the movie magazines
and newspapers started printing my picture and giving me
write-ups. I used to tell lies in my interviews—chiefly about
my mother and father. I'd say she was dead—and he was
somewhere in Europe. I lied because I was ashamed to have
the world know my mother was in a mental institution
—and that I had been born "out of wedlock" and never
heard my illegal father's voice.

I finally straightened these lies out, and I was surprised
at the way the magazines and newspapers treated my "new
confessions." They were kind and none of them picked on
me.

Just as I was beginning to go over with the public in a big
way, I got word that my "nude calendar" was going to be
put on the market as a Marilyn Monroe novelty. I thought
this would push me into the cold again. A writer I met
laughed at my tears.

"The nude calendar is going to put you over with the
biggest bang the town has heard in years," he said. "The
same thing happened in the 20s to a girl who was on the
verge of movie fame. She couldn't quite seem to excite the
movie-queen-makers of the studios. She was called
unphotogenic and 'good for a small part but definitely not
star material.' "

"Like me," I said.

"Yes," the writer said. "Then one day a studio official
giving a party got hold of a two-reel film in which the girl
had performed. The film was intended for rental to stag

parties. In the picture this young girl danced entirely in the nude. The dance was also vulgar and suggestive. As a result every movie producer or director who saw the stag film became haunted with the nude performer. They vied for her services as if she were the only female on tap, and the only full set of secondary female characteristics in Hollywood. She became famous in a few months and is still famous today [and one of my worst detractors]."

It turned out very much like that for me, too. Everybody in the studio wanted me as a star in his movie. I finally went into *Gentlemen Prefer Blondes*, and after that, *How to Marry a Millionaire*. I liked doing these pictures. I liked the fact that I was important in making them a great financial success and that my studio cleaned up a fortune, despite that its chief had considered me unphotogenic. I liked the fact that the movie salesmen who came to Hollywood for a big studio sales rally whistled loudest and longest when I entered their midst.

I liked the raise I finally received to twelve hundred a week. Even after all the deductions were taken from my salary it remained more money a week than I had once been able to make in six months. I had clothes, fame, money, a future, all the publicity I could dream of. I even had a few friends. And there was always a romance in the air. But instead of being happy over all these fairytale things that had happened to me I grew depressed and finally desperate. My life suddenly seemed as wrong and unbearable to me as it had in the days of my early despairs.

29

WHY I AM
A HOLLYWOOD MISFIT

I HAVE many bad social habits. People are always lecturing me about them. I am invariably late for appointments—sometimes as much as two hours. I've tried to change my ways but the things that make me late are too strong—and too pleasing.

When I have to be somewhere for dinner at eight o'clock, I will lie in the bathtub for an hour or longer. Eight o'clock will come and go and I still remain in the tub. I keep pouring perfumes into the water and letting the water run out and refilling the tub with fresh water. I forget about eight o'clock and my dinner date. I keep thinking and feeling far away.

Sometimes I know the truth of what I'm doing. It isn't Marilyn Monroe in the tub but Norma Jean. I'm giving Norma Jean a treat. She used to have to bathe in water used by six or eight other people. Now she can bathe in water as clean and transparent as a pane of glass. And it seems that Norma can't get enough of fresh bath water that smells of real perfume.

There's another thing that helps to make me "late." After I get out of the tub I spend a long time rubbing creams into my skin. I love to do this. Sometimes another hour will pass, happily.

When I finally start putting my clothes on I move as slowly as I can. I begin to feel a little guilty because there seems to be an impulse in me to be as late as possible for my dinner date. It makes something in me happy—to be late.

People are waiting for me. People are eager to see me. I'm wanted. And I remember the years I was unwanted. All

the hundreds of times nobody wanted to see the little servant girl, Norma Jean—not even her mother.

I feel a queer satisfaction in punishing the people who
are wanting me now. But it's not them I'm really punishing.
It's the long ago people who didn't want Norma Jean.

It isn't only punishment I feel. I get thrilled as if I were
Norma Jean going to a party and not Miss Monroe. The
later I am the happier Norma Jean grows.

People dislike me for such tardiness. They scold me and
explain to me it's because I want to seem important and
make a spectacular entrance. That's partly true, except it's
Norma that longs for importance—and not me.

My social faults such as this one, and also not being able
to laugh all the time at parties as if I were swooning with
joy, or not being able to keep chattering like a parrot to
other parrots—seem less important to me than some social
faults I notice in others.

The worst thing that happens to people when they dress
up and go to a party is that they leave their real selves at
home. They're like people on a stage playing somebody
else. They play that they're important, and they want you to
meet their importance, not themselves. But worse than that
is the fact that when people are being "social" they don't
dare be human or intelligent. They don't dare to think
anything different than the other people at the party. The
men and women are not only dressed alike but their minds
become all alike. And they expect everybody at the party to
say only "party things."

I freeze up when I see people making important faces at
me, or when I notice them strutting among the lesser
party-lights. I like important people, but I like them when
they're doing important things—not just collecting a few
bows from lesser guests.

In party society there are also people who are unable to
feel important—even if it's an important party and their
names are going to be in the movie columns the next
morning in "among those present." These people usually

just mill around like extras on a movie set. They don't seem to have any lines or any "business" except to be ornamental space fillers.

But I can't feel sorry for them because the minute I join one of these extra-groups they all start chattering like mad and laughing and saying things that nobody can understand. I feel that having found someone more ill at ease than themselves—me—they're out to impress me what a gay and intimate time they're having.

Hollywood parties not only confuse me, but they often disillusion me. The disillusion comes when I meet a movie star I've been admiring since childhood.

I always thought that movie stars were exciting and talented people full of special personality. Meeting one of them at a party I discover usually that he (or she) is colorless and even frightened. I've often stood silent at a party for hours listening to my movie idols turn into dull and little people.

30

MY OWN RECIPE
FOR FAME

THERE ARE three different ways of becoming famous in the movies. The first way more often happens to men than to women. It happens suddenly as the result of a single performance in a movie.

An actor will go along getting jobs and doing good work and getting nowhere. Then all of a sudden, like John Garfield long ago or Kirk Douglas, Marlon Brando, Jose Ferrer, more recently—he will appear as a lead in a picture and wake up after the reviews as star for the rest of his life.

Occasionally this also happens to an actress, but the occasions haven't been recent. The actress usually becomes a star in two other ways. The first way is the Studio Buildup. When the Front Office is convinced that one of their contract players has star possibilities in her, a big campaign is started. The Star Possibility is surrounded by various teachers and coaches. Word is sent out to all the Producers in the Studio that the Possibility is the biggest coming box-office attraction in the industry. And all the producers in the studio start fighting to get her as the lead for one of their pictures.

In the meantime the publicity department goes to work on the Star Possibility and floods the press, the wire services, and the magazines with stories about her wonderful character and fascinating oddities and thousands of photographs.

The columnists are bombarded with announcements about the possibilities of every sort, from a half dozen impending marriages to an equal number of starring vehicles.

Pretty soon the whole country gets the impression that nearly all the eligible romantic males of the land are trying to marry the Possibility and that she is going to appear in half the important movies produced in Hollywood.

All this takes a great deal of money and powerful efforts on everybody's part except the young actress on whose brow the Studio has decided to weld a silver star.

The other way to fame open to the actress is the way of scandal. Sleep with a half dozen famous Don Juans, divorce a few husbands, get named in police raids, café brawls or other wives' divorce suits, and you can wind up almost as much in demand by the movie producers as a Bette Davis or Vivien Leigh.

The only trouble with becoming famous as a result of a half dozen scandalous happenings is that the scandal-made star can't just rest on her old scandals. If she wants to keep her high place in the public eye and on the Hollywood producer's casting list she has to keep getting into more and more hot water. After you're thirty-five getting into romantic hot water is a little difficult, and getting yourself publicized in love triangles and café duels over your favors needs not only smart press agents but also a little miracle to help out.

I became famous in the movies in none of these three accepted ways. The studio never thought of me as a Star Possibility, and the notion of putting me in as a lead on a picture was as far from Mr. Zanuck's head as of handing me over his Front Office as a dressing room. It would make a very good one.

Thus I didn't get a chance to burst upon the public as a Great Talent.

And there was no Studio campaign or buildup. I was never groomed. The press and the columnists were kept in ignorance of my existence. No telegrams and other passionate Front Office communiqués went out about me to the Sales Force or the nation's exhibitors.

And there was no scandal to my name. The calendar business came after I was already famous everywhere except in Mr. Zanuck's mind and in the plans of my Studio, 20th Century-Fox.

I had been terrified for a week before the news of my calendar nude broke. I was sure that it would put an end to my fame and that I would be dropped by the studio, press, and public and never survive my "sin." My sin had been no more than I have written—posing for the nude picture because I needed fifty dollars desperately to get my automobile out of hock.

There are many other ways for a young and pretty girl to make fifty dollars in Hollywood without any danger of being "exposed." I guess the public knew this. Somehow the story of the nude calendar pose didn't reflect scandal on me. It was accepted by the public for what it was, a ghost out of poverty rather than sin risen to haunt me.

A few weeks after the story became known I realized that far from hurting me in any way it had helped me. The public was not only touched by this proof of my honest poverty a short time ago, but people also liked the calendar—by the millions.

To return to my unorthodox rise to movie fame, it came about entirely at the insistence of the movie public, and most of this movie public was in uniform in Korea, fighting.

Letters started flooding my studio by the thousands and hundreds of thousands. They were all addressed to me. They came at the rate of thirty-five hundred a week, and then five and seven thousand a week.

I received five times more mail than the studio's top box-office star of the time, who was Betty Grable.

Reports from the mail room confused the Front Office. The Publicity Department was called in and asked if its personnel were engaged in some secret campaign in my behalf. There was none. The letters were pouring in only because moviegoers had seen me on the screen and felt excited enough to write and thank me or ask for my photograph.

News that the public was hailing me as the new Hollywood movie favorite appeared in the Hollywood gossip columns. No one sent the news out. The columnists printed it because people were talking about it.

The Studio officials remained unimpressed for a time. They had their own Star Possibilities they were plugging. I was regarded from Mr. Zanuck down as a sort of freak who for no reason anybody could put a finger on was capturing some morbid side of the public's fancy.

I was making three hundred dollars a week and spending most of it on lessons, dancing and singing lessons and acting lessons. I lived in a small single room and was as broke as I used to be when I had no regular job. I had to borrow ten and twenty dollars every week or so. The difference was now that I could pay my debts back quicker—sometimes inside of the same week.

Finally the mail from the movie fans got to be so fantastic in quantity that the Front Office could no more ignore me than it might an earthquake that was tipping Mr. Zanuck's desk over. I was sent for by Mr. Zanuck himself, looked at briefly, and given a few mumbled words of advice.

All I had to do, Mr. Zanuck said, was to trust him. He would do everything that was best for me and help me to become a big star for the studio.

I could tell that Mr. Zanuck didn't like me very much and that he still couldn't see any more talent or beauty in me than when he had fired me a year before on the general grounds of being unphotogenic. Studio Bosses are very jealous of their powers. Like political bosses they like to pick out their own candidates for greatness. They don't like the Public rising up and dumping an unphotogenic entry in their lap and saying, "She's our girl."

There was some normal fumbling with how to handle me, in what sort of pictures to put me. And there was still a deep conviction in the Studio's bosom that I was only a flash in the pan and would very likely be forgotten in a year.

It wasn't to happen that way. I knew it at the time. I knew what I had known when I was thirteen and walked along the sea edge in a bathing suit for the first time. I knew

I belonged to the Public and to the world, not because I was talented or even beautiful but because I had never belonged to anything or anyone else. The Public was the only family, the only Prince Charming and the only home I had ever dreamed of.

When you have only a single dream it is more than likely to come true—because you keep working toward it without getting mixed up.

I worked hard and all day long. I worked inside the studio and outside it. It wouldn't be long now, I knew, before Mr. Zanuck would give me a lead in a big picture. The Publicity Department was already on the ball. The magazines seemed to be celebrating a perpetual Marilyn Monroe week. My picture was on nearly all their covers.

People began to treat me differently. I was no longer a freak, a sort of stray ornament, like some stray cat, to invite in and forget about. I was becoming important enough to be attacked. Famous actresses took to denouncing me as a sure way of getting their names in the papers.

In fact my popularity seemed almost entirely a masculine phenomenon. The women either pretended that I amused them or came right out, with no pretense, that I irritated them.

I did nothing vulgar on the screen. And I did nothing vulgar off the screen. All I did was work from eight to fourteen hours a day either acting or trying to improve my talents.

I felt tired all the time. Worse, I felt dull. The colors seemed to have gone out of the world. I wasn't unhappy and I didn't lie awake nights crying and hanging my head. That sort of thing was over—at least for now.

What happened was that in working to make good I had forgotten all about living. There was no fun anymore in anything. There was no love in me for anything or anyone. There was only success—beginning.

And then one night a friend at the Studio said, "A fellow like him. He's Joe DiMaggio."

"I've heard of him," I said.

It was partly true. I knew the name but I didn't actually know what it stood for.

"Don't you know who he is?" my friend asked.

"He's a football or baseball player," I said.

"Wonderful," my friend laughed. "It's time you were coming out of your Marilyn Monroe tunnel. DiMaggio is one of the greatest names that was ever in baseball. He's still the idol of millions of fans."

"I don't care to meet him," I said. Asked why, I said that I didn't like the way sports and athletes dressed, for one thing.

"I don't like men in loud clothes," I said, "with checked suits and big muscles and pink ties. I get nervous."

But I went to join a small party with whom Joe DiMaggio was having dinner in Chasen's Restaurant.

31

A GENTLEMAN
FROM
CENTER FIELD

I T WAS A balmy night, and I was late as usual.

When the dinner host said, "Miss Monroe, this is Joe DiMaggio," I was quite surprised. Mr. Joe DiMaggio was unexpected.

I had thought I was going to meet a loud, sporty fellow. Instead I found myself smiling at a reserved gentleman in a gray suit, with a gray tie and a sprinkle of gray in his hair. There were a few blue polka dots in his tie. If I hadn't been told he was some sort of a ball player, I would have guessed he was either a steel magnate or a congressman.

He said, "I'm glad to meet you," and then fell silent for the whole rest of the evening. We sat next to each other at the table. I addressed only one remark to him.

"There's a blue polka dot exactly in the middle of your tie knot," I said. "Did it take you long to fix it like that?"

Mr. DiMaggio shook his head. I could see right away he was not a man to waste words. Acting mysterious and far away while in company was my own sort of specialty. I didn't see how it was going to work on somebody who was busy being mysterious and far away himself.

I learned during the next year that I was mistaken about this baseball idol. Joe wasn't putting on an act when he was silent, and he was the least far away man I had ever known. It was just his way of being on the ball.

But to return to my first meal with Mr. DiMaggio—he didn't try to impress me or anybody else. The other men talked and threw their personalities around. Mr. DiMaggio just sat there. Yet somehow he was the most exciting man at the table. The excitement was in his eyes. They were sharp and alert.

Then I became aware of something odd. The men at the table weren't showing off for me or telling their stories for my attention. It was Mr. DiMaggio they were wooing. This was a novelty. No *woman* had ever put me so much in the shade before.

But as far as I was concerned, Mr. DiMaggio was all novelty. In Hollywood, the more important a man is the more he talks. The better he is at his job the more he brags. By these Hollywood standards of male greatness my dinner companion was a nobody. Yet I had never met any man in Hollywood who got so much respect and attention at a dinner table. Sitting next to Mr. DiMaggio was like sitting next to a peacock with its tail spread—that's how noticeable you were.

I had been dead tired when I arrived. Now suddenly I wasn't tired anymore. There was no denying I felt attracted. But I couldn't figure out by what. I was always able to tell what it was about a man that attracted me. Except this time with Mr. DiMaggio.

My feelings for this silent smiling man began to disturb me. What was the use of buzzing all over for a man who was like somebody sitting alone in the Observation Car?

Then I began to understand something. His silence wasn't an act. It was his way of being himself. And I thought, "You learn to be silent and smiling like that from having millions of people look at you with love and excitement while you stand alone getting ready to do something."

Only I wished I knew what it was Mr. DiMaggio did. I tried to remember what the football players did the time Jim Dougherty took me to a football game. I couldn't recall anything interesting.

I had never seen a baseball game; so there was no use trying to figure out what a baseball player did that was important. But I was sure now it was something. After one hour all the men at the table were still talking for Mr. DiMaggio's benefit.

Men are a lot different than women in this respect. They

are always full of hero worship for a champion of their sex. It's hard to imagine a table full of women sitting for a whole hour flattering and wooing another woman if she were three champions.

Since my remark about the blue polka dot there had been no further conversation between my dinner partner and me. Even though I was attracted I couldn't help thinking, "I wonder if he knows I'm an actress? Probably not. And I'll probably never find out. He's the kind of egomaniac who would rather cut off an arm than express some curiosity about somebody else. The whole thing is a waste of time. The thing to do is to go home—and forget him—and without delay."

I told the host I was tired and had a hard day ahead at the studio. It was the truth. I was playing in a movie called *Don't Bother to Knock*.

Mr. DiMaggio stood up when I did.

"May I see you to the door?" he asked.

I didn't discourage him.

At the door he broke his silence again.

"I'll walk you to your car," he said.

When we got to my car he made an even longer speech.

"I don't live very far from here, and I haven't any transportation," he said. "Would you mind dropping me at my hotel?"

I said I would be happy to.

I drove for five minutes and began to feel depressed. I didn't want Mr. DiMaggio to step out of the car and out of my life in another two minutes, which was going to happen as soon as we reached his hotel. I slowed down to a crawl as we approached the place.

In the nick of time Mr. DiMaggio spoke up again.

"I don't feel like turning in," he said. "Would you mind driving around a little while?"

Would I mind! My heart jumped, and I felt full of happiness. But all I did was nod mysteriously and answer, "It's a lovely night for a drive."

We rode around for three hours. After the first hour I

began to find out things about Joe DiMaggio. He was a baseball player and had belonged to the Yankee Ball Club of the American League in New York. And he always worried when he went out with a girl. He didn't mind going out once with her. It was the second time he didn't like. As for the third time, that very seldom happened. He had a loyal friend named George Solotaire who ran interference for him and pried the girl loose.

"Is Mr. Solotaire in Hollywood with you?" I asked.

He said he was.

"I'll try not to make him too much trouble when he starts prying me loose," I said.

"I don't think I will have use for Mr. Solotaire's services this trip," he replied.

After that we didn't talk for another half hour, but I didn't mind. I had an instinct that compliments from Mr. DiMaggio were going to be few and far between, so I was content to sit in silence and enjoy the one he had just paid me.

Then he spoke up again.

"I saw your picture the other day," he said.

"Which movie was it?" I asked.

"It wasn't a movie," he answered. "It was a photograph of you on the sports page."

I remembered the one. The Studio had sent me out on a publicity stunt to Pasadena where some team from Chicago called The Sox was clowning around getting ready for the eastern baseball season. I wore rather abbreviated shorts and a bra, and the ball players took turns lifting me up on their shoulders and playing piggyback with me while the publicity men took photographs.

"I imagine you must have had your picture taken doing publicity stunts like that a thousand times," I said.

"Not quite," Mr. DiMaggio answered. "The best I ever got was Ethel Barrymore or General MacArthur. You're prettier."

The admission had an odd effect on me. I had read reams on reams of writing about my good looks, and scores of men had told me I was beautiful. But this was the first time my heart had jumped to hear it. I knew what that meant, and I began to mope. Something was starting between Mr. DiMaggio and me. It was always nice when it started, always exciting. But it always ended up in dullness.

I began to feel silly driving around Beverly Hills like a prowl car.

But it wasn't silly.

T HE STUDIO was always thinking up ways for me to get more publicity. One of the ways they thought up was for me to lead the parade in Atlantic City of the Miss America contest bathing beauties. I wasn't to compete but to function as some sort of an official.

Everything went well until the U.S. Armed Forces stepped in. The Armed Forces also run a publicity department. A publicity officer wanted to know if I would like to help the Armed Forces in their campaign to recruit Wacs, Waves, and Spars to serve Uncle Sam.

I said I would love to do that.

The next day a Publicity Photograph was arranged. I stood surrounded by a Wac, Wave, and Spar. They were good-looking girls, and they were dressed in uniforms. I, on the other hand, not being in any military service, couldn't very well wear a uniform. I wore one of my regular afternoon dresses. Joe hadn't yet won his argument about the neckline.

It was an entirely decent dress. You could ride in a street car in it without disturbing the passengers.

But there was one bright-minded photographer who figured he would get a more striking picture if he photographed me shooting down. I didn't notice him pointing his camera from the balcony a few feet above me. I posed for the camera in front of us.

The next day brought the scandal. The "shooting down" photograph had been condemned by some army general. He said it would be bad for the Armed Services for parents to think their daughters might be subjected to the influences of somebody like me—who showed her bosom in public.

I thought this a little mean. I hadn't meant to show my bosom, and I hadn't been aware of the camera that was peeping down under my bodice.

Of course nobody would believe me.

Earl Wilson, who writes about bosoms in the New York *Post* interviewed me over the telephone.

"Come now, Marilyn," he said, "didn't you lean forward for that shot?"

I said I hadn't. It was the photographer who had leaned downward.

I felt silly about the whole thing. It was surprising that a woman's bosom, slightly revealed, could become a matter of national concern. You would think that all the other women kept their bosoms in a vault.

I didn't mind the publicity too much although I felt I had outgrown the cheesecake phase of my movie career. I was hoping now that some of my other talents might be recognized.

The bad thing about cheesecake publicity is the letters you get from cranks. They are often frightening.

The letter writer cuts out just the bosom of your photograph and writes dirty words across it and mails it to you—without his signature. Or maybe her signature. And there are worse insults and depravities thrown at you by Mr. and Mrs. Anonymous.

A WISE MAN
OPENS
MY EYES

HE MOST brilliant man I have ever known is Michael Chekhov, the actor and author. He is a descendant of Anton Chekhov, the great Russian dramatist and story writer. He is a man of great spiritual depth. He is selfless and saintlike and witty, too. In Russia he was the best actor they had. And in Hollywood in the half dozen movies he played, he was considered superb. There was no character actor who could hold a candle to Michael Chekhov—who could play clown and Hamlet, and love interest, half as wonderfully. But Michael retired from the screen. The last picture in which he played was *Specter of the Rose* in which his performance was hailed as brilliant.

In his home Michael devoted himself to writing, gardening, and teaching acting to a few people. I became one of them.

As Michael's pupil, I learned more than acting. I learned psychology, history, and the good manners of art—taste.

I studied a dozen plays. Michael discussed their characters and the many ways to play them. I had never heard anything so fascinating as my teacher's talk. Every time he spoke, the world seemed to become bigger and more exciting.

One afternoon Michael and I were doing a scene from *The Cherry Orchard*. To set a scene with Michael Chekhov in his house was more exciting than to act on any movie set I had known. Acting became important. It became an art that belonged to the actor, not to the director or producer, or the man whose money had bought the studio. It was an art that transformed you into somebody else, that increased your life and mind. I had always loved acting and tried hard to learn it. But with Michael Chekhov, acting became more than a profession to me. It became a sort of religion.

In the midst of our scene from *The Cherry Orchard*, Michael suddenly stopped, put his hand over his eyes for a moment, and then looked at me with a gentle grin.

"May I ask you a personal question?" he asked.

"Anything," I said.

"Will you tell me truthfully," Michael asked again. "Were you thinking of sex while we played that scene?"

"No," I said, "there's no sex in this scene. I wasn't thinking of it at all."

"You had no half thoughts of embraces and kisses in your mind?" Michael persisted.

"None," I said. "I was completely concentrated on the scene."

"I believe you," said Michael, "you always speak the truth."

"To you," I said.

He walked up and down a few minutes and said, "It's very strange. All through our playing of that scene I kept receiving sex vibrations from you. As if you were a woman in the grip of passion. I stopped because I thought you must be too sexually preoccupied to continue."

I started to cry. He paid no attention to my tears but went on intently. "I understand your problem with your studio now, Marilyn, and I even understand your studio. You are a young woman who gives off sex vibrations—no matter what you are doing or thinking. The whole world has already responded to those vibrations. They come off the movie screens when you are on them. And your studio bosses are only interested in your sex vibrations. They care nothing about you as an actress. You can make them a fortune by merely vibrating in front of the camera. I see now why they refuse to regard you as an actress. You are more valuable to them as a sex stimulant. And all they want of you is to make money out of you by photographing your erotic vibrations. I can understand their reasons and plans."

Michael Chekhov smiled at me.

"You can make a fortune just standing still or moving in front of the cameras and doing almost no acting whatsoever," Michael said.

"I don't want that," I said.

"Why not?" he asked me gently.

"Because I want to be an artist," I answered, "not an erotic freak. I don't want to be sold to the public as a celluloid aphrodisical. Look at me and start shaking. It was all right for the first few years. But now it's different."

This talk started my fight with the studio.

I realized that just as I had once fought to get into the movies and become an actress, I would now have to fight to become myself and to be able to use my talents. If I didn't fight I would become a piece of merchandise to be sold off the movie pushcart.

I kept telephoning the studio begging for an interview with its chief. I was told, "No interview—just appear on the set when you're notified."

I stayed in my room alone and talked to myself. They were ready to give me a lot of money—a million if I would marry them and never wander off and fall in love with art. I hadn't wanted Johnny Hyde's million, and Johnny was a much sweeter and kinder character than 20th Century-Fox. I decided I didn't want the studio's million, either. I wanted to be myself and not just a freak vibration that made fortunes for the studio sex peddlers.

I HAVE to be careful in writing about my husband Joe DiMaggio because he winces easily. Many of the things that seem normal or even desirable to me are very annoying to him.

He dislikes being photographed or interviewed. If he is even so much as asked to participate in some publicity stunt he registers a big explosion.

Joe doesn't mind being written about, but he is against doing anything to encourage or attract publicity. In fact, publicity is something that makes him wince more than anything else.

Publicity was one of the problems in our courtship after the three-hour tour of Beverly Hills that first night.

"I wonder if I can take all your crazy publicity," Joe said.

"You don't have to be part of it," I argued.

"I am," he said. "And it bothers me."

"It's part of my career," I said. "When you were a baseball idol you didn't duck photographers."

"Yes, I did," he answered.

"I can't," I said.

"Don't I know it," Joe nodded.

"Do you want me to hide in a basement?" I asked.

"We'll see how it works out," he said.

There were a number of things to "work out." One was the low neckline of my dresses and suits.

I gave in on this one. I wear no more low-cut dresses. Instead they have a sort of collar. The neckline is an inch under my chin.

I put up an argument about the neckline for some time.

But after my adventure with the Army in the Atlantic City Beauty Contest, I began to think that Joe might be right in his "show them nothing" stand.

The situation at the Studio seemed to grow worse everyday. I mean every time I thought about it, it looked worse to me.

Among the black marks the front office had against me was the fact that I had kept Mr. Zanuck waiting for an hour at an Award Presentations ceremony. He accused me of doing it on purpose. This wasn't true. I was working on the set, and it took me an hour to get the makeup off and my hair restored to normal.

But keeping Mr. Zanuck waiting was only a side issue in the trouble that kept growing. Even the matter of getting more money was a side issue—to me as well as to the Studio. When a studio stumbles on to a box-office name in its midst, it means millions of dollars income. And every studio has learned to be very considerate, financially, toward the goose who lays their golden eggs—as long as she keeps laying them, at least.

The trouble was about something deeper. I wanted to be treated as a human being who had earned a few rights since her orphanage days.

When I had asked to see the script of a movie in which it was announced I was going to star, I was informed that Mr. Zanuck didn't consider it necessary for me to see the script in advance. I would be given my part to memorize at the proper time.

The name of the movie was *The Girl in Pink Tights*. It was a remake of an old Betty Grable story.

The title made me nervous. I was working with all my might trying to become an actress. I felt that the studio might cash in on exhibiting me in pink tights in a crude movie, but that I wouldn't.

I notified the studio that I couldn't agree to play in *Pink Tights* until after I had read the script—and liked it. And I went to San Francisco where Joe lived.

The Studio's first reply was to put me on suspension and take me off the payroll. I didn't mind. Their next move was to take me off suspension and put me back on salary. I didn't mind that either.

Then a copy of *The Girl in Pink Tights* script arrived. I read that and that I minded.

It was much worse even than I had been afraid it would be. Movie musicals usually had dull stories. This one was way below dullness. It was silly—even for a movie about the 1890s.

I had to play the character of a prim, angrily virtuous school teacher who decided to become a sort of hoochy-koochy dancer in a Bowery dive so as to earn enough money to put her fiancé through medical college. The fiancé is high up in society with a dowager ma, but they are shy on money. This dreary cliché-spouting bore in pink tights was the cheapest character I had ever read in a script.

What's the use of being a star if you have to play something you're ashamed of? When I thought of Joe or any of my friends seeing me on the screen as this rear-wiggling school teacher doing bumps and grinds in the great cause of medicine I blushed to my toes.

Pink Tights didn't even get to marry the Society Man for whose sake she unveiled herself to wiggle in a Bowery Dive. She married instead the owner of the Dive—a man of rough appearance but with a heart of gold (or mush) underneath!

I sent back word to the Studio that I didn't like the script and wouldn't play in the movie.

I heard from different people that nobody in the Studio liked the script. Even Mr. Zanuck's conviction that it was a masterpiece about humble but colorful people had been shaken somewhat by one of his star directors refusing to shoot it.

But that didn't help my case any. Everybody in the world could despise the picture, including, finally, its audience, and I would still remain in the wrong. This was because of my standing in the eyes of the Front Office. In these eyes I was still a sort of freak performer who had made good against its better judgment.

I wasn't angry but it made me sad. When the rest of the world was looking at someone called Marilyn Monroe, Mr. Zanuck, in whose hands my future rested, was able to see only Norma Jean—and treat me as Norma Jean had always been treated.

Joe and I had been talking about getting married for some months. We knew it wouldn't be an easy marriage. On the other hand we couldn't keep on going forever as a pair of Cross-country Lovers. It might begin to hurt both our careers.

The public doesn't mind people living together without being married, providing they don't overdo it. It would be very odd of the public if it did mind since, according to Dr. Kinsey in his report on such things, eighty per cent of all married women have had premarital real love experiences with their husbands.

After much talk Joe and I had decided that since we couldn't give each other up, marriage was the only solution to our problem. But we had left time and place in the air.

One day Joe said to me:

"You're having all this trouble with the Studio and not working so why don't we get married now? I've got to go to Japan anyway on some baseball business, and we could make a honeymoon out of the trip."

That's the way Joe is, always cool and practical. When I get excited over some magazine giving me a big picture spread, he grins and sneers a little.

"Yes, but where's the money?" he asks.

"It's the publicity," I yell back.

"Money is better," he says in the quiet way men use when they think they have won an argument.

And so we were married and took off for Japan on our honeymoon.

That was something I had never planned on or dreamed about—becoming the wife of a great man. Anymore than

Joe had ever thought of marrying a woman who seemed eighty per cent publicity.

The truth is that we were very much alike. My publicity, like Joe's greatness, is something on the outside. It has nothing to do with what we actually are. What I seem to Joe I haven't heard yet. He's a slow talker. What Joe is to me is a man whose looks, and character, I love with all my heart.

Y TRAVELS have always been of the same kind. No matter where I've gone or why I've gone there, it ends up that I never see anything. Becoming a movie star is living on a merry-go-round. When you travel you take the merry-go-round with you. You don't see natives or new scenery. You see chiefly the same press agent, the same sort of interviewers, and the same picture layouts of yourself.

I thought Japan would be different because the Studio had wiped its hands of me. The Publicity Department had received instructions to spike all Monroe publicity. I was to be given the don't-mention-her-name treatment.

Joe was very happy to hear this, but he didn't stay happy long. From the minute the Studio washed its hands of me, my name started popping out of big front page headlines. Joe's too.

Seeing your name in front page headlines as if you were some kind of a major accident or gun battle is always startling. No matter how often you see it you don't get used to it. You keep thinking—"That's about me. The whole country's reading about me. Maybe the world is."

And you remember things. All your hungry days and hysterical nights step up to the headlines and take a bow.

Japan turned out to be another country I never saw. An Army officer came up to our seat in the airplane as we were approaching Japan. He was General Christenberry. After introducing himself, he asked, "How would you like to entertain the soldiers in Korea?"

"I'd like to," my husband answered, "but I don't think I'll have time this trip."

"I wasn't asking you," the General said. "My inquiry was directed at your wife."

"She can do anything she wants," said Joe. "It's her honeymoon."

He grinned at me and added, "Go ahead."

Joe stayed in Tokyo, and I went to Korea. My first stop was in a hospital full of wounded soldiers. I sang some songs including one called, "Do It Again."

The soldiers were wonderful. They cheered and applauded as if they were having a good time. Everybody loved everything I did except the officer in charge of my Korean tour. He took me aside and told me I would have to change my material.

"What material?" I asked.

"That song, 'Do It Again,'" he said. "It's too suggestive to sing to soldiers. You'll have to do a classy song instead."

"But 'Do It Again' is a classy song," I told him. "It's a George Gershwin song."

"Doesn't matter," the officer insisted. "You'll have to change it."

I hadn't sung the song with any suggestive meaning. I had sung it as a straight, wistful love song. But I knew there was no use arguing about it. I'd been up against this sort of thing before. People had a habit of looking at me as if I were some kind of a mirror instead of a person. They didn't see me, they saw their own lewd thoughts. Then they white-masked themselves by calling me the lewd one.

"If I change the phrase, 'do it again,' to 'kiss me again,' will that be all right?" I asked.

The officer was dubious, but he finally agreed.

"Try it," he said, "and try not to put any suggestive meaning into it."

"Just kissing," I said.

We took a helicopter for the front. I didn't see Korea and its battlefields and beaten up towns. I left one landing field and came down on another. Then I was put in a truck and taken to where the 45th Division was waiting. The 45th

Division was my first audience after the wounded in the hospital.

It was cold and starting to snow. I was backstage in dungarees. Out front the show was on. I could hear music playing and a roar of voices trying to drown it out.

An officer came back stage. He was excited.

"You'll have to go on ahead of schedule," he said. "I don't think we can hold them any longer. They're throwing rocks on the stage."

The roar I'd been hearing was my name being yelled by the soldiers.

I changed into my silk gown as quickly as I could. It had a low neckline and no sleeves. I felt worried all of a sudden about my material, not the Gershwin song but the others I was going to sing—"Diamonds Are A Girl's Best Friend."

It seemed like the wrong thing to say to soldiers in Korea, earning only soldiers' pay. Then I remembered the dance I did after the song. It was a cute dance. I knew they would like it.

*

This is where Marilyn's manuscript ended when she gave it to me.

MILTON H. GREENE

The End